Dmitry Shostakovi

Titles in the series Critical Lives present the work of leading cultural figures of the modern period. Each book explores the life of the artist, writer, philosopher or architect in question and relates it to their major works.

In the same series

Antonin Artaud *David A. Shafer*
Roland Barthes *Andy Stafford*
Georges Bataille *Stuart Kendall*
Charles Baudelaire *Rosemary Lloyd*
Simone de Beauvoir *Ursula Tidd*
Samuel Beckett *Andrew Gibson*
Walter Benjamin *Esther Leslie*
John Berger *Andy Merrifield*
Leonard Bernstein *Paul R. Laird*
Joseph Beuys *Claudia Mesch*
Jorge Luis Borges *Jason Wilson*
Constantin Brancusi *Sanda Miller*
Bertolt Brecht *Philip Glahn*
Charles Bukowski *David Stephen Calonne*
Mikhail Bulgakov *J.A.E. Curtis*
William S. Burroughs *Phil Baker*
John Cage *Rob Haskins*
Albert Camus *Edward J. Hughes*
Fidel Castro *Nick Caistor*
Paul Cézanne *Jon Kear*
Coco Chanel *Linda Simon*
Noam Chomsky *Wolfgang B. Sperlich*
Jean Cocteau *James S. Williams*
Joseph Conrad *Robert Hampson*
Salvador Dalí *Mary Ann Caws*
Guy Debord *Andy Merrifield*
Claude Debussy *David J. Code*
Gilles Deleuze *Frida Beckman*
Fyodor Dostoevsky *Robert Bird*
Marcel Duchamp *Caroline Cros*
Sergei Eisenstein *Mike O'Mahony*
William Faulkner *Kirk Curnutt*
Gustave Flaubert *Anne Green*
Michel Foucault *David Macey*
Mahatma Gandhi *Douglas Allen*
Jean Genet *Stephen Barber*
Allen Ginsberg *Steve Finbow*
Johann Wolfgang von Goethe *Jeremy Adler*
Günter Grass *Julian Preece*
Ernest Hemingway *Verna Kale*
Langston Hughes *W. Jason Miller*
Victor Hugo *Bradley Stephens*
Derek Jarman *Michael Charlesworth*
Alfred Jarry *Jill Fell*
James Joyce *Andrew Gibson*
Carl Jung *Paul Bishop*
Franz Kafka *Sander L. Gilman*
Frida Kahlo *Gannit Ankori*
Søren Kierkegaard *Alastair Hannay*

Yves Klein *Nuit Banai*
Arthur Koestler *Edward Saunders*
Akira Kurosawa *Peter Wild*
Lenin *Lars T. Lih*
Pierre Loti *Richard M. Berrong*
Rosa Luxemburg *Dana Mills*
Jean-François Lyotard *Kiff Bamford*
René Magritte *Patricia Allmer*
Stéphane Mallarmé *Roger Pearson*
Thomas Mann *Herbert Lehnert and Eva Wessell*
Gabriel García Márquez *Stephen M. Hart*
Karl Marx *Paul Thomas*
Guy de Maupassant *Christopher Lloyd*
Herman Melville *Kevin J. Hayes*
Henry Miller *David Stephen Calonne*
Yukio Mishima *Damian Flanagan*
Eadweard Muybridge *Marta Braun*
Vladimir Nabokov *Barbara Wyllie*
Pablo Neruda *Dominic Moran*
Georgia O'Keeffe *Nancy J. Scott*
Octavio Paz *Nick Caistor*
Pablo Picasso *Mary Ann Caws*
Edgar Allan Poe *Kevin J. Hayes*
Ezra Pound *Alec Marsh*
Marcel Proust *Adam Watt*
Arthur Rimbaud *Seth Whidden*
John Ruskin *Andrew Ballantyne*
Jean-Paul Sartre *Andrew Leak*
Erik Satie *Mary E. Davis*
Arnold Schoenberg *Mark Berry*
Arthur Schopenhauer *Peter B. Lewis*
Dmitry Shostakovich *Pauline Fairclough*
Adam Smith *Jonathan Conlin*
Susan Sontag *Jerome Boyd Maunsell*
Gertrude Stein *Lucy Daniel*
Stendhal *Francesco Manzini*
Igor Stravinsky *Jonathan Cross*
Rabindranath Tagore *Bashabi Fraser*
Pyotr Tchaikovsky *Philip Ross Bullock*
Leo Tolstoy *Andrei Zorin*
Leon Trotsky *Paul Le Blanc*
Mark Twain *Kevin J. Hayes*
Richard Wagner *Raymond Furness*
Alfred Russel Wallace *Patrick Armstrong*
Simone Weil *Palle Yourgrau*
Tennessee Williams *Paul Ibell*
Ludwig Wittgenstein *Edward Kanterian*
Virginia Woolf *Ira Nadel*
Frank Lloyd Wright *Robert McCarter*

Dmitry Shostakovich

Pauline Fairclough

REAKTION BOOKS

For Richard, with love

Published by Reaktion Books Ltd
Unit 32, Waterside
44–48 Wharf Road
London N1 7UX, UK
www.reaktionbooks.co.uk

First published 2019, reprinted 2020
Copyright © Pauline Fairclough 2019

Printed and bound in Great Britain by Bell & Bain, Glasgow

A catalogue record for this book is available from the British Library

ISBN 978 1 78914 127 6

Contents

Prelude: Writing About Shostakovich 7

1 'She did not wait for me' 13
2 On the Edge of the Whirlwind 37
3 Civic Responsibility and Self-assertion 65
4 Finding a Way Forward 95
5 The Inner Gaze 116
6 Final Years 150
   Postlude 174

References 178
Select Bibliography 187
Acknowledgements 190
Photo Acknowledgements 191

Shostakovich in 1962.

Prelude: Writing About Shostakovich

There is no shortage of books about Dmitry Shostakovich. Since his death in 1975 he has had the dubious privilege of becoming one of the last century's most mythologized and fought-over cultural icons. His posthumous reputation has been trapped in a cycle of Cold War-fuelled prejudice (represented by those who found his music anachronistic) and equally Cold War-fuelled defence (portraying him as a misunderstood dissident). Now the Cold War is far behind us, and the prejudice against Shostakovich's accessible musical language that went with it is waning, debates over Shostakovich's music, personality and political views are no longer fought with such ideological passion. However, they have not entirely died out. The vested interests are no longer political – that potent blend of Western belief in its own cultural superiority and hatred of the Soviet regime – but are instead those of commercial media: especially of a classical music media that feels continually imperilled by funding cuts and audience apathy. The more the 'tragic Shostakovich' image is stoked, the more marketable he is. Much as Soviet music journalists used to try and engage proletarian audiences with tales of Beethoven's revolutionary fervour, today music presenters and even professional performers use identical tactics to shock and impress us with Shostakovich's political relevance. Invariably this relevance is displayed via the now-familiar narratives of misery: Shostakovich's hounding by Stalin, the coded dissidence in his music, the irresistibly romantic image of a composer all but destroyed by the Communist regime he was forced to serve. To audiences who, like their Soviet counterparts in the 1920s, might think of classical music as boring and irrelevant, the subliminal message is clear: once we have told you how much this composer suffered under one of the cruellest dictators of the last century, you'll be a lot more interested in his music.

Perhaps it would be perverse to take serious issue with this marketing strategy; for whatever our interest in Shostakovich, surely any introduction to his music can only be a good thing? As someone who teaches music in universities for a living, I am always pleased to discover how popular Shostakovich's music continues to be. Yet so often his popularity is accompanied by expressions of pity: considering that we are nearly thirty years on from the 'official' end of the old Cold War, the classic Western view of Shostakovich as oppressed by Stalinism is surprisingly robust. By seeing Shostakovich this way, we miss many things about both the composer himself and the society that produced him. For example, it is true that the Bolshevik Revolution of 1917 prompted a mass exodus of writers, musicians and composers from Russia. Yet many brilliant creative and philosophical minds remained behind, and Shostakovich always worked in a culture that was rich in artistic talent. Even when we consider Shostakovich's career in a fully global context, considering him alongside his peers in other countries, it is clear that he knew, and worked with, some of the greatest artists in the world, just as it is clear that he himself was one of the most significant composers of the last century. It is of course true that Shostakovich suffered from political repression; but to conclude that this had a negative impact on his music immediately places us on shaky ground when we consider how popular it has been all over the world. We might well hesitate to conclude that Stalinism 'warped' or otherwise damaged his creative voice when we reflect that the work he produced at the height of Stalin's political terror – his Fifth Symphony – is one of the most frequently played twentieth-century symphonies in the modern-day orchestral repertoire.

Immediately after Shostakovich's death in 1975, however, the most powerful influence upon Shostakovich's Western image was not music education or the media: it was the Cold War itself. No one has had a bigger stake in this than his self-styled amanuensis, Solomon Volkov. When, in early 1979, he walked into the New York music publishers Harper & Row with a manuscript he claimed was the dictated memoirs of the recently deceased composer, he held out the promise of something ineffably precious to the Western side of the Cold War: evidence that the Russians' greatest cultural icon had lived all his life in hatred and fear of Soviet power. Once the book, *Testimony*, was published, those who had been inclined to sneer at Shostakovich for his Soviet citizenship were able to pity him instead; those who were already aware of the distorted image Shostakovich had been forced to present to the West were unsurprised; and those most deeply immersed in Shostakovich's own culture recognized that something was amiss.[1] Parts of it were plagiarized from much earlier publications, thus throwing Volkov's 'dictated memoirs' story into doubt. Anyone wishing to follow the twists and turns of the post-*Testimony* saga may consult the authoritative source, showing facsimile pages of the original manuscript and corresponding passages from Soviet journals.[2]

This short Prelude is not the place to go into what used to be called the 'Shostakovich Wars'; a few moments on an Internet search engine will instantly throw up websites and sources of varying reliability where the curious reader can easily find evidence of how contentious a figure Shostakovich has been, and continues to be. But it does need to be said, perhaps, that writing a biography of this fought-over composer requires certain positions to be taken, lines drawn and personal inclinations made clear. Like that of most music-lovers in the Western world, my introduction to Shostakovich was politicized right from the start: he was presented to me as a persecuted composer trapped in the frightening and repressive world of Soviet Russia. Even decades after the collapse of the Soviet Union, this is still how many of us 'discover' Shostakovich: as a tragic victim. And this is an image easily reinforced by listening to the music: the grieving slow movement of the Fifth Symphony, penned at the height of the Stalinist terror; the suicide note of the Eighth Quartet, composed after Shostakovich was pressurized into joining the Communist Party; the valedictory final works. But is this an accurate image, or one shaped overwhelmingly by Western Cold War, anti-Soviet sentiment?

My answer to this question is that this image is not completely inaccurate, but it is very, very partial. Shostakovich was not, as his funeral oration pompously put it, 'a loyal son of the Communist Party'. But we too easily extrapolate from that that he would have preferred to have lived in the 'free' West, where he could have composed the music he 'really' wished to write; and that is nothing but a Western fantasy of breathtaking presumption. Shostakovich travelled frequently to Western countries from 1949 onwards. And though he was an interested traveller who enjoyed seeing new places, he did not like everything he saw in the 'free West'. During his trip to Edinburgh for the Festival in 1962, for instance, he was taken to the private estate of Lady Rosebery and was deeply shocked by the personal wealth and privilege displayed to him. Nor was he dazzled by the self-styled post-war avant-garde, in any of its manifestations: he liked some of the music, but was sceptical about what he perceived as its ivory-tower retreat into a high modernism that alienated ordinary music-lovers. Writing for a wide population was in Shostakovich's DNA, and not simply because it was branded on him by Stalinism; he wished to communicate through his music, and was pleased when audiences responded to it warmly. He felt his career was a calling, which imposed specific ethical and civic duties on him, and far from wishing to escape those obligations, he took them extremely seriously; we might even say that he was sustained by them. To see his entire career – or even just the part of it following the attacks on him in 1936 – as compromised, or an artistic failure, is as insulting to Shostakovich as it is gratifying to the Cold-War-warrior mindset. It is true that Shostakovich's career was shaped by social forces that differed from those in capitalist democracies in the same period: the Soviet state did indeed operate along broad lines of 'he who pays the piper calls the tune'. But when dealing with a composer of Shostakovich's stature, the resulting music is powerful enough to defy glib assumptions that he 'watered down' or otherwise compromised his 'natural' style.

My own 'lines drawn' are, I hope, straightforward ones. Though I have not been squeamish about interpreting Shostakovich's music in places, I have no wish to insist on any particular reading: pieces of music are in any case rarely 'about' one single message or image. There are as many ways to hear this music as there are listeners, and my way is just one of those. I do not wish to 'prove' that Shostakovich had a particular set of political beliefs, since I can only guess at what these might have been. In placing interpretations on particular works, I have been guided by events around them and, where possible, by Shostakovich's responses, either in letters or in the memoirs of people around him. If I had any particular personal angle on my subject, it was to challenge the idea, still commonly held, that Shostakovich's music is depressing, and that he himself was a broken man at the end of his life. This popular image is still widely asserted: it can be found in the British *Classic FM* online composer profile of Shostakovich, and even where this belief is not stated as fact, it can be forcefully implied, most recently in Julian Barnes's novel *The Noise of Time*, where Barnes continually compares the old Shostakovich to his younger self as though they were entirely different people. However, the biographical record of Shostakovich's last years, patchy though it is, does not support this image. Though he was undeniably depressed by illness in the last few years of his life, the surviving letters and testimony of friends suggest strongly that Shostakovich's essential personality never changed: he kept both his iron grip on his incredible talent and his keen sense of humour to the very end of his life.

In writing this book, I have been continually guided by the work of three remarkable scholars: Olga Digonskaya, the Chief Archivist of the Shostakovich Archive in Moscow, the cellist and writer Elizabeth Wilson and Laurel Fay, the leading Shostakovich scholar outside Russia. Their decades of meticulous fact-finding and rich experience have helped make the world of Shostakovich research the powerhouse that it is today, all sustained in Russia by Shostakovich's widow, Irina Antonovna Shostakovich, who runs the Shostakovich Archive and founded the DSCH publishing house that is still issuing the New Collected Works Edition of Shostakovich's music. Thanks to them, and to the work of many other musicians, writers and scholars, Shostakovich's legacy is still unfolding, whether through newly discovered letters, lost manuscripts or archival discoveries. There is still a huge amount potentially to be discovered, not least his old NKVD/KGB file, which must be preserved somewhere, and to which no scholar has yet had access. Russian archives are not so easily accessible now as they were in the heady days of the post-1991 era, but the discoveries keep coming: Shostakovich is still surprising us decades after his death. This biography takes account of the most up-to-date Shostakovich scholarship available at the time of writing, including that in Russian.

1

'She did not wait for me'

By the time Dmitry Shostakovich graduated from the Leningrad Conservatoire in the summer of 1929 he already had a dizzying array of professional successes behind him. He had composed two symphonies, the first of which had been performed worldwide and praised by leading composers and conductors of the day, including Alban Berg and Gustav Mahler's former protégé, Bruno Walter. Aged just 22, he commanded enough authority to have persuaded Samuil Samosud, chief conductor of Leningrad's Maly Theatre, to stage his audacious opera *The Nose*, a work that outstripped even Berg's *Wozzeck* in difficulty on almost every level: vocal, instrumental and theatrical. He had written two film scores (*New Babylon* and *Alone*), been commissioned to compose incidental music for Moscow's leading stage director Vsevolod Meyerhold (*The Bedbug*) and composed a ballet (*The Golden Age*). He was able to call luminaries of Russia's opera, theatre, literary and music worlds his personal friends, and had a burgeoning address list of writers, critics, musicians, artists and dancers with whom he was on either good professional terms, or in some cases personally intimate.

How was it that this youth – still immature in his personal relationships, living at home with his mother and sisters and suffering at times exceedingly poor health – bestrode the early Soviet cultural scene with such astonishing authority? And how could such a fragile figure even have survived the harsh conditions of the Civil War period (1918–21), which saw the wholesale flight of the Russian intelligentsia, along with them a great many distinguished musicians and composers, from Russia's starving and terrorized cities? Between the Bolshevik Revolution of October 1917 and the end of the Civil War Russia had lost Serge Rachmaninoff, Sergey Prokofiev, Jascha Heifetz, Gregor Piatigorsky, Vladimir Horowitz, Serge Koussevitsky and countless others. Even among those who did not leave Russia itself, many sought temporary shelter in the provinces while life in the new Bolshevik capital of Petrograd was especially hard. Shostakovich, only just turned eleven when Lenin became Russia's leader, had to make his way in an environment that was unimaginably tough. As the bitter fighting between Bolshevik forces and the 'White' opposition tore Russia apart, even the day-to-day business of survival hung in the balance. No one in Shostakovich's family had enough to eat; his father's salary was worth little in the years of rampant inflation and their rented apartment was turned into a *kommunalka* (the enforced communal living conditions after the Revolution, whereby family apartments were divided into single-room living quarters, housing several families with shared facilities).

Shostakovich survived, even thrived, but no one could claim that his life, in that first decade after 1917, was easy. No one's was. Yet the mystery of his early professional success, and his incredible personal connections, becomes easier to understand when we consider the close networks of Russia's pre-revolutionary intelligentsia. First, Shostakovich's parents – incomers to St Petersburg from Siberia – were themselves well connected before the Revolution. They had a wide group of friends in the city; they were relatively wealthy, entertained often, and Shostakovich's mother Sofia Vasilievna had graduated from the Conservatoire as a pianist. The three Shostakovich children, Maria, Dmitry and Zoya, attended prestigious local schools where they rubbed shoulders with children from influential families; this was how the young

Shostakovich became so friendly with the much older Russian artist Boris Kustodiev, who sketched him on several occasions (Shostakovich kept Kustodiev's portrait of him on his wall throughout his life). But the family had several political advantages after 1917 too: Shostakovich's father Dmitry Boleslavovich had not been called up to fight in 1914 because of his own family's revolutionary past, and his brother-in-law Maxim Kostrikin was a prominent Bolshevik whose grandmother had been personal friends with Lenin's own mother. They also seem to have been remarkably pragmatic with regard to the loss of their domestic space and privacy after the Bolshevik Revolution: rather than wait to have strangers moved in, the Shostakovich family swiftly arranged to share their apartment with selected friends-of-friends and were thus spared the fate of many former well-to-do families who found themselves ignominiously shunted into cordoned-off spaces in their own homes. From what we know of their attitudes to the February Revolution in 1917, which replaced Tsarist rule with a Provisional Government, both of Shostakovich's parents welcomed the fall of the monarchy; his mother and aunt took part in the memorial procession for those who had died in that uprising, processing through the Petrograd streets to the Field of Mars and singing the nineteenth-century song 'You Fell as Victims'.

As the power struggles between revolutionary forces continued through 1917, Shostakovich, who had been learning the piano for just two years, was already giving his first concerts and starting to compose. It was after his mother and aunt's participation in the memorial procession that he composed his 'Funeral March in Memory of the Victims of Revolution', thus rather ironically beginning his career with the kind of political statement that he would spend most of his adult life trying to avoid. Thanks to his mother's connections at the Conservatoire, he was admitted at the startlingly young age of thirteen, in 1919, with the support of its director, Alexander Glazunov. Though he was still attending ordinary school (his sisters' gymnasium), he left a year later without even a leaving certificate, apparently defeated by mathematics. Thereafter Shostakovich's education would be entirely musical, though the fact that he was admitted on both performance and composition courses, and at a very young age, meant an enormous workload. His numbered surviving compositions from these early years – the Scherzo in F sharp minor, five of his Eight Preludes, *Theme and Variations*, *Two Fables of Krïlov* and *Three Fantastic Dances* for piano – show a rapid acceleration in confidence and technique. His composition teacher, Maximilian Steinberg, had to help him with the orchestration of his Scherzo, with the result that it sounds distinctly Tchaikovskian. But by the time he was writing his *Fables*, tension between his old role models (initially Musorgsky's song cycle *In the Nursery*) and his own voice was producing a skittish role play between old and new influences; and the playful elegance of the *Fantastic Dances* shows the new (though short-lived) presence of Debussy in Shostakovich's musical armoury.

Throughout these early student years the Shostakovich family had relied on their breadwinner, Dmitry Boleslavovich. Though he was fortunate to find decent work under the Bolshevik regime, his income had fallen in value with extreme inflation and the family had adjusted to a substantial drop in living standards. Suddenly, in mid-February 1923, he died after a brief illness. The family was plunged into direst poverty overnight: Shostakovich's mother, who had never been in paid work, took a menial clerical job as well as giving piano lessons in return for food, but it was not sufficient for a family of three children. As though that were not enough, Shostakovich became ill soon afterwards with tuberculosis of the lymphatic system, a horrible and potentially life-threatening condition more commonly known as scrofula, which is generally caused by malnutrition and poor living conditions. Terrified of losing her son as she had lost a sister to the disease, Shostakovich's mother arranged for an operation and sold the family piano in order to pay for his convalescence that summer in the Crimea, accompanied by his older sister Maria. By this time Shostakovich, despite his recent operation to remove the lumps on his neck, had succeeded in graduating from the Conservatoire as a pianist, stoically performing his graduation recital with his neck wrapped in bandages. As we can glean from his letters from the Crimea at this time, his mother's fear was matched only by his own delight in his first taste of freedom – and his first experience of romance.

The summer of 1923 marked a turning point in Shostakovich's life. For there in the Crimea, aged just seventeen and relatively unchaperoned, he met a girl of his own age, Tatiana Glivenko, and fell in love with her. Their feelings for each other were to be a source of both delight and confusion over the next decade as they continued their relationship through correspondence upon their return to their respective homes in Leningrad and Moscow (they shared one further summer on the Black Sea in 1926). Naturally, Shostakovich's sister told their mother all about the relationship, evidently prompting some maternal anxiety, which Shostakovich sought to soothe as best he could:

> Mother dear, I want to warn you that if I ever fall in love, maybe I won't want to marry. But if I did get married and if my wife ever fell in love with another man, I wouldn't say a word; and if she wanted a divorce I would give her one and I would blame only myself . . . But at the same time there exists the sacred calling of a mother and father. So you see, when I really start thinking about it my head starts spinning. Anyhow, love is free![1]

His words can be seen as reflecting the then-fashionable ideas of the Bolshevik feminist politician Alexandra Kollontai, who argued that the institution of marriage was responsible for the exploitation of women. However, Shostakovich evidently does not go so far as Kollontai, who believed that raising children was a chief

Dmitry Boleslavovich Shostakovich, the composer's father.

Sofia Vasilievna Shostakovich, the composer's mother.

component of this exploitation, and advocated handing over child-rearing to the State. At the impressively young age of seventeen, Shostakovich was already sympathetic to the new feminist ideas of his time, but could not relinquish his own childhood memories of a beloved father, the security of a loving home or his own wish to have a family, which would become very strong indeed over the coming years. Nothing encapsulates Shostakovich's conflicted personal relationship with the Communist regime in its early years better than these musings on the pros and cons of the nuclear family. Coming from a protected, materially secure family himself, he would always attach intense value to a stable domestic life, which could be seen as quintessentially bourgeois (as indeed the pre-1917 Shostakovich family was). But at the same time he was alert and receptive to fresh ideas about how Soviet society should be structured and had no wish to dominate a future partner. These half-formed thoughts would turn out to be curiously prescient, not only in the immediate future, as the tangled threads of Shostakovich's romantic relationships led him towards his eventual marriage in 1932, but in the very nature of his first marriage, in which his assertions to his mother proved to be far from empty words.

After an abortive attempt to finish his education at the Moscow Conservatoire in the spring of 1924 – prompted by dissatisfaction with his Leningrad teachers, an unpleasant attempt to deprive him of Glazunov's financial support from jealous fellow students and a gratifying encounter with Moscow's leading musicians and teachers – Shostakovich at last qualified as a composer from Steinberg's undergraduate class. His graduation piece was the First Symphony, which he had completed the previous July, to his teacher's far from clear-cut approval. Though we might see Shostakovich as a youthful iconoclast, enjoying older composers' horror at his talent for the grotesque, in fact disappointing Steinberg and Glazunov caused him only distress. One of his most important Moscow friends, the

Tatiana Glivenko, Shostakovich's first girlfriend.

music theorist Boleslav Yavorsky, proved a loyal confidant at a time when Shostakovich was unsure of where to turn. In a letter dated 16 April 1925 to this older friend, we see not the arrogance of youth so much as an explosion of frustration:

> I would like to write to them: 'To my dear teachers, Alexander Konstantinovich [Glazunov], Nikolay Alexandrovich [Sokolov], Maximilian Oseevich [Steinberg] and Leonid Vladimirovich [Nikolaev]! Thank you for teaching me music craftsmanship. Thank you, Maximilian Oseevich, for teaching me to fear parallel octaves and teaching me how to avoid them. Thank you, Nikolay Alexandrovich, for teaching me how to unite two themes, and for teaching me how to write bad fugues. Thank you, Leonid Vladimirovich, for teaching me piano technique

and how to learn difficult passages by heart. And thank you, Alexander Konstantinovich, for all that went on under your vigilant watch. And now give me my freedom. Let me listen to the voice which comes from inside me, and don't force me to unquestioningly accept what I hear you tell me. There shall be no musical servitude . . . Give me my freedom!'[2]

That Shostakovich completed his symphony at all, given the difficulties he and his family endured during the year of its composition (1924–5) seems nothing short of miraculous. From November 1924 he began working as a cinema pianist to help his mother make ends meet, an exhausting job that sapped his energies. Worse, in June 1925 Shostakovich suffered his second bereavement: his closest friend Vladimir (Volodya) Kurchavov died from tuberculosis in the Crimea. The loss hit Shostakovich hard: the two friends lived through several months of knowing that the end was coming. Midway through composing the symphony's finale while in Moscow, Shostakovich wrote to another friend, his piano classmate Lev Oborin: 'Volodya is dying, darkness surrounds me . . . From sheer misery I've started to compose the finale of the Symphony. It's turning out pretty gloomy.'[3] It was not the first time Shostakovich had responded to personal sorrow by composing – his Suite for Two Pianos was begun immediately on return from his father's funeral – but while that earlier work was dedicated to his father's memory, Shostakovich dedicated his First Symphony to another Moscow friend, Mikhail Kvadri, with whom he had a slightly uneasy on-and-off friendship even at the point at which he made the dedication. The slow movement and finale seem permeated with grief, and are strikingly prescient of Shostakovich's mature style: the arresting timpani solos midway through the finale are close pre-echoes of those ushering in the harrowing final act of his opera *Lady Macbeth of Mtsensk*, which he would begin in October 1930, but complete only in December 1932. In the slow movement Shostakovich's mature symphonic voice – even that of the wartime Seventh and Eighth Symphonies – is already strongly present. Both in details of its orchestration (especially the writing for woodwind) and in its ability to capture a particular kind of frozen stillness, we clearly hear the future composer of the Eighth Symphony's slow movement. It was a work of astonishing maturity and self-assertion by a composer who had endured great personal loss and hardship, and it would amaze the experienced musicians who heard in it the powerfully original 'voice from inside' that Shostakovich had longed to express freely. The symphony's first champion, the conductor Nikolay Malko, would not only perform it repeatedly in Russia, but abroad too – as would Bruno Walter, Otto Klemperer and Arturo Toscanini, to name just a few of Shostakovich's early supporters. The date of the symphony's Leningrad premiere, 12 May 1926, would be a celebrated date for Shostakovich all his life.

Between finishing the symphony in April 1925 and starting his postgraduate studies in 1926, Shostakovich experienced a hiatus in his creative energies of over a year's duration, possibly caused by a combination of emotional exhaustion and a need to establish his independence, despite remaining Steinberg's postgraduate student until 1929. When at last he resumed composing later in 1926, he embarked on a three-year bout of staggering productivity, using a radically altered language. A flurry of avant-garde music poured from him in waves of release from pent-up frustration with the staid Conservatoire teaching he had long since outgrown: the First Piano Sonata, his Second Symphony, 'To October', and his dazzling first opera *The Nose*. Steinberg's diary entry after hearing *The Nose* ('terrible rubbish') more than accounts for Shostakovich's insurmountable frustration with his teacher. But even Shostakovich's piano teacher Lev Nikolaev, on hearing him perform the sonata, sniffed that it was 'a sonata for metronome to the accompaniment of piano', which gives us a good indication of

Shostakovich soon after finishing his First Symphony, June 1925.

how older musicians would react to the motoric devices that were becoming more prominent in Shostakovich's music.[4] For the source of Shostakovich's dry, 'running-on-the-spot' music, we have to look away from his Russian models of Tchaikovsky and Musorgsky and turn westwards, to the music of Paul Hindemith and Shostakovich's Westernized former compatriot Sergey Prokofiev. In a questionnaire set by the musicologist Roman Gruber dating from 1927 to 1928, Shostakovich lists Hindemith as one of his favourite composers, and specifically his Concerto for Orchestra as one of his favourite works.[5] And that key influence can clearly be heard in Shostakovich's Second Symphony which, despite its revolutionary title ('To October') and setting of proletarian verses at the end, is a thoroughly modernist work. In a bold avant-garde gesture, Shostakovich announced the entry of the chorus with a drum stroke and siren combination, a sound effect copied directly from the ending of Hindemith's Concerto for Orchestra. Because the symphony was a commission to celebrate the ten-year anniversary of the October Revolution, and because Soviet composers were expected to engage proletarian audiences and not simply write 'bourgeois' music for the middle classes, Shostakovich was defensive about its complexity. He claimed in a letter to Yavorsky (2 July 1927) that before its first performance he had tried out the work on 'four workers and a peasant':

> Popov told you that the texture sounds terribly complicated. That's not true. The music is simple and accessible to ordinary people . . . I gathered together five people, who don't know my music at all, and played it to them . . . they didn't understand all of it, because I played badly, but they went into ecstasies about the choral part and tried to sing along.[6]

Although Shostakovich thought the verses by the proletarian poet Alexander Bezïmensky were atrocious, he set them inventively, using a combination of melodic choral writing and declamation: at the end of the symphony the choir shout out 'October! The commune! And Lenin!' And though overall the symphony's language was complex, it was also clearly descriptive, opening with inchoate, murky grumblings in the bass (signalling pre-1917 gloom), moving ultimately to an obviously victorious major-key peroration.

Even as he was working on the Second Symphony in the spring of 1927, Shostakovich was planning his first opera. He chose a subject that was both baffling and ingenious: Nikolay Gogol's eccentric short story 'The Nose', about a pompous government official and man-about-town (Major Kovalëv) who awakes one morning to find his nose has disappeared. In the catalogue of absurdity that follows, Kovalëv pursues his own nose (now disguised as a high-ranking civil servant) through St Petersburg, is roundly snubbed by the offending organ in the process, attempts to report it to the local paper, mourns the impossibility of continuing his planned courtship, and then, when it seems all hope is lost, awakes again to find his nose back in place and his world put to rights. To really understand why choosing Gogol's tale was so radical, it is worth pausing to consider Russian operatic precedents: Tchaikovsky's settings of Pushkin (*Eugene Onegin*, *The Queen of Spades*), historical epics (Tchaikovsky's *The Oprichniki*, Musorgsky's *Boris Godunov* and *Khovanshchina*) and a whole series of fairy-tale operas (Rimsky-Korsakov's *The Snow Maiden* and *The Golden Cockerel*, to name just two). Though there had been relatively lightweight precursors – even Musorgsky wrote a comic opera (*Sorochinsky Fair*) – no one had composed a full-blown farce for the serious opera stage. *The Nose* lacked any political content, whereas other Soviet composers were already attempting to create a new type of 'Soviet' opera such as Vasily Zolotarev's *Dekabristy* and the jointly composed *Red Petrograd* by Arseny Gladkovsky and Yevgeny Prussak, both staged in 1925. Shostakovich completely sidestepped the Soviet present and favoured comic farce over epic or heroic content.

Nevertheless, the music directors of the Maly Theatre had enough faith in Shostakovich to go ahead with a premiere. This fact is even more remarkable when we consider the inauspicious year of its staging: 1930. Leningrad's musical life was deeply divided by then, with a group of very aggressive proletarian composers taking it upon themselves to police musical institutions from the Conservatoires down to amateur choirs, purging them, where they could, of 'bourgeois' elements such as former church deacons, unsuitable repertoire (such as Rachmaninoff's music) and, above all, any form of light music and jazz. Their principal targets were light music entertainers, émigré composers, church music and composers whom they regarded as their rivals in publishing, radio and music education. Shostakovich was not really a target for this group, whom he had placated with scores for workers' theatricals at the Theatre for Working-class Youth in Leningrad, and a shamelessly hypocritical statement published in the paper *Proletarian Musician* in March 1930, calling for the eradication of gypsy music, foxtrot and jazz from the musical sphere. That his avowed disapproval was insincere is plain, not only from his evident sympathy with these genres, which he would use time and time again in his ballets, but from the fact that gypsy music was a type of light music especially close to Shostakovich's heart. His father had often sung such songs at home, and both in his youth and old age Shostakovich never lost his love for these sentimental romances. In short, his 'affiliation' with the proletarians, such as it was, was at least in part opportunistic. Moreover, it did not save *The Nose* from their approbation. Nor did the fact that, when given the obligatory trials before workers' audiences (who were surveyed with questionnaires), the opera received – probably to Shostakovich's own surprise – 100 per cent approval.[7] Shostakovich himself believed that a truly fresh audience, as opposed to one used to attending operas at the Bolshoy, would enjoy *The Nose*, declaring hyperbolically that 'I . . . count naturally on the worker and peasant spectator. If I am not comprehensible to them I should be deported.'[8] Unfortunately, proletarian critics proved immune to these defensive strategies. *The Nose* was labelled a product of 'infantile sickness of leftism' and, after fourteen performances between January and June 1930, was taken off the stage and not played again in Russia until 1974, the year before the composer's death.

Considering Shostakovich's defensiveness with regard to the complexity of his Second Symphony, it is curious that his Third, the 'First of May', is not obviously easier on the ear. Written mostly on holiday in the summer of 1929, it was both part of the portfolio of works Shostakovich had to submit for his postgraduate qualification and also a clear declaration of both ideological 'correctness' and personal ambition. We know that the final choral conclusion – setting another low-quality political text, this time by Semën Kirsanov – was composed after the main body of the symphony and that Shostakovich had initially hoped that the prominent proletarian poet Demyan Bedny would provide the text instead. But though both these early symphonies are habitually categorized as 'avant-garde' Shostakovich, the composer himself, clearly aimed to capture the popular tunes and styles of the late 1920s (mass songs, marches and such like) in a way that was both audible and recognizable without compromising on technical virtuosity. In consequence, Shostakovich more or less realized his ambition of composing a symphony that does the exact opposite of what any symphony traditionally does: not a single theme is developed aside from a few reminiscences, so fleeting that most listeners will miss them.

While the Second Symphony had been a commission, and its political content set more or less in stone by the fact that it was composed as a celebration work for the tenth anniversary of the October Revolution, the Third was composed in complete freedom. Aside from ideological commitment or personal ambition,

Shostakovich could have felt under no pressure to have produced another work with a political message. So what were Shostakovich's political beliefs at this point in his life? A letter to his girlfriend Tatiana Glivenko gives us a small clue as to what Shostakovich's feelings about the Bolsheviks may have been in the pre-Stalin era. Writing in early 1924 about the plans to bury Lenin in Moscow, the eighteen-year-old composer confided, 'I'm sad, Tanechka, very sad. I'm sad that V. I. Lenin has died and that I will not be able to say farewell to him because he is being buried in Moscow. The Petrograd Soviet applied to have his body moved to Petrograd, but this application must have been refused.'[9] At this stage in his life, Shostakovich was an open and frank correspondent and there is no reason not to take his words at face value. The personal hardships he and his family had suffered as a result of the Bolshevik takeover seem not to have affected his personal feelings towards the radical new society he found himself living in. On the contrary, Shostakovich gave every indication of finding that new society an inspiring place to live and work. Professional pressures that frustrated musicians at this time, such as the increase in militant groups seizing power from the traditional bastions of musical privilege – the Moscow Conservatoire was even briefly renamed after the Bolshevik Commissar Felix Kon in these difficult years – were not directly attributable to government. In time Stalin was to step in and close down the infighting, briefly winning musicians' gratitude in so doing. Meanwhile Shostakovich played the system for all he was worth, securing lucrative and high-profile commissions and premieres, pleasing the proletarian critics with his ideological offerings (in which category we can also place his two ballet scores of this period, *The Golden Age* and *The Bolt*), while fully indulging his brief passion for avant-garde techniques in other works. His Third Symphony was benignly received, but all the same, after a few performances it vanished from orchestral programmes and was only revived much later in the composer's life.

While Shostakovich's professional life proceeded rather bumpily in these difficult years of musical infighting, his personal relationships were also painfully unsatisfactory. The one shining light during the late 1920s was his new friendship with the legendary polymath and music critic Ivan Sollertinsky, which dates properly from the summer of 1927. This would be a lifelong friendship, founded – as few, if any, of his earlier relationships had been – on a true meeting of minds and an unshakeable mutual respect. Often oversensitive, even paranoid, in his youthful friendships, Shostakovich's letters to Sollertinsky show a new quality of deep trust and confidence. They also give us insights into Shostakovich's character that are not shown anywhere else, especially in the early stages of their correspondence, when he still expressed himself very frankly and at length. As Sollertinsky's second wife Irina Derzayeva recalled, 'When they didn't manage to meet, Shostakovich would usually ring up . . . They were simply in love, and didn't conceal their delight in each other.'[10] Though Sollertinsky was an important creative influence on Shostakovich, perhaps above all in sharing with him his passion for Mahler's music, his friendship also provided him with the emotional support the composer badly needed. Shostakovich was himself a very loyal and affectionate friend, but the wholeheartedness he brought to his relationships meant that he easily felt bruised and rejected. With Sollertinsky, their mutual adoration was never questioned, and so their friendship not only provided Shostakovich with emotional reassurance, but opened up a new world of youthful debauchery and fun in which, however, confidences about more serious personal issues could be made in the knowledge that neither would indulge in gossip (something of a tall order for Sollertinsky, according to Shostakovich himself).[11]

Writing dolefully to Sollertinsky from Odessa in the summer of 1930, Shostakovich confessed: 'I envy you. You have a rich personal life. And mine, in general, is shit.'[12] Given that Sollertinsky's secretive first marriage to the ballerina we know only as 'Vera' was in trouble and would shortly come to an end, Shostakovich's envy seems misplaced. But its source was Shostakovich's own bitter realization that he had probably allowed his greatest chance of domestic happiness to slip through his fingers. Tatiana Glivenko, apparently tired of Shostakovich's indecision regarding their future, had married in February 1929. Though Shostakovich was then courting the woman he would later marry, Nina Varzar (whom he had met in the summer of 1927), early in 1930 he had gone to Moscow to persuade Tatiana to leave her husband, apparently encouraged by her own complaints about him and their marriage. As late as 1931 Shostakovich, now actually engaged to Nina, tried to make Tatiana jealous by pretending that he, too, had got married. In reality he and Nina were due to marry in December 1931, but Shostakovich failed to appear at the registry office, apparently still unsure whether he should commit himself or not (this apparently being precisely what Tatiana had found exasperating about him). None of his strategies had any effect other than to upset both Tatiana and himself. He launched a final last-ditch attempt to win Tatiana back in early 1932, sending his sister Maria to Moscow to beg her to come back to Leningrad and live with Shostakovich – only to be told that this was now out of the question. Tatiana was pregnant, and her baby was born in May 1932. For Shostakovich, this ended the whole affair. He would willingly attempt to disrupt a marriage – Soviet marriage vows were not sacred ones, and divorce was both common and easy to obtain at that time – but he would not break up a family. Two weeks later he and Nina went again to the registry office, and this time Shostakovich went through with it.

Thus when, in 1930, Shostakovich expresses deep discontent with his love life, it is not hard to understand why. But one further anecdote from this period of romantic instability is crucial for helping us understand later events in Shostakovich's life. During the summer of 1930, mooning over his lost love and feeling

Nina Varzar, early 1930s.

lonely, Shostakovich struck up a holiday romance in the Black
Sea, the details of which he confided to Sollertinsky. Two girls
had approached him as he dined with friends in a restaurant,
asking him if he was Shostakovich; hugely flattered, the 24-year-
old composer scented romantic potential and indulged in a little
under-the-table groping. After spending a few more days together,
Shostakovich learned that the friend of his beloved 'Rozochka'
(Rozalia) had been arrested for prostitution and was, in fact,
well known for it in the Black Sea resorts. Staff at Shostakovich's
hotel warned him to be careful, as did the conductor Alexander
Gauk, who was with Shostakovich in Odessa. Initially convinced,
and resolved not to get further involved, when he saw Rozalia
unexpectedly in the restaurant, he reported wryly to Sollertinsky,
'I almost burst into tears with joy and love' – and thereafter, it
seems, continued seeing her. A week later Shostakovich confessed
that he had actually promised to marry Rozalia and got as far as
the registry office, only to discover that their marriage could not go
ahead without certain documents, which Shostakovich, whether by
accident or design, had failed to bring with him. He signs off with
an air of worldly wisdom: 'How are your family affairs? Let this be a
lesson to you: don't marry. I'm single and it's fine', probably feeling
that he had had a narrow escape.[13]

This absurd incident shows that, where women were concerned,
Shostakovich was hopelessly impulsive and easily swayed. He was
hesitating before taking the momentous step of marriage (for so
he clearly felt it was, despite the ease of divorce), felt he had already
made a terrible mistake in procrastinating too long over Tatiana,
and was not yet sure that Nina was the right woman for him. At the
same time he looked enviously, and admiringly, at Sollertinsky's
apparent popularity with women. He liked to pretend that he was
an experienced man of the world, successful with women and
sexually confident, but in fact his letters show that he was the
precise opposite: he was emotionally vulnerable, easily led and

prone to sudden and drastic romantic decisions. In this respect Shostakovich's character was deeply rooted and did not change even when he was much older. As we can clearly see in his bizarre and short-lived second marriage in 1956, his anxiety about being single, and his failure to judge romantic situations reliably, came back to the fore once he found himself again alone, despite the far higher stakes involved, since this second wife would have to be stepmother to his two children.

The final work of this early period, composed over an untypically long period of time for him – 1928–32 – is one very seldom performed: the *Six Romances on Verses by Japanese Poets*, which Shostakovich eventually dedicated in its entirety to Nina. He wrote the first three songs, which he offered to Nina there and then in 1928; the fourth song was composed in 1931 and he wrote the last two, and orchestrated the whole set, while completing his opera *Lady Macbeth* in 1932. The *Japanese Romances* encapsulate a unique set of circumstances, both in Soviet cultural life and in Shostakovich's own personal life. Initially the impetus to write them seems to have been prompted by the visit of a Japanese cultural delegation in 1927, and his acquaintance (through Sollertinsky) with one member in particular, Narumi Kandzo, who stayed in Leningrad for nine years after this visit. The first three songs were all settings of a well-known collection of old Japanese poetry, published in translation by Alexander Brandt in 1912 and first set by Stravinsky, whose own *Three Japanese Lyrics* (1913) were well known in Shostakovich's circle. The first three songs, 'Love', 'Before Suicide' and 'An Immodest Glance' are all darkly tinged, but the cycle takes an even more melancholy turn with the fourth song from 1931, 'For the First and Last Time', about a consummated love affair. The text for this song was not actually Japanese at all, but was very probably, as the scholar Galina Kopïtova has surmised, based on a poem by Rabindranath Tagore, 'The Gardener', which had first been published in Russia in 1914, and which Sollertinsky knew well. Soviet interest in Tagore was at a peak at this time: a collection of his works was translated into Russian and published in 1926, and the poet himself spent two weeks in the Soviet Union in September 1930, prompting a flurry of interest in his poetry and painting; his poems were also widely printed in Soviet cultural magazines and journals. The textual changes transform the addressee of Tagore's poem – 'O world' – to a girl ('my darling'): 'I plucked your flower, my darling/ I held you to my breast/ I become as one with you/ When the night had passed, I saw/ That you were no longer with me/ Only the pain remained.'[14] The autograph manuscript for this song is dated 29 November 1931, just days before Shostakovich failed to turn up for his marriage to Nina. A letter to his mother from 30 June 1931, probably reflecting on the loss of Tatiana, reads dramatically,

> I condemned myself to death. Circumstances seem stronger than me, stronger than my creations, stronger than my will . . . I, evidently, was born under an unlucky star. My path in life, notwithstanding the fact that I am not yet 25, has crashed blindly. I have not the strength to live.[15]

But if the fourth song reads like a lament for Tatiana, the last two songs (settings from the 1923 Russian translation of classical Japanese poetry by N. Konrad) leave yet more questions hanging over Shostakovich's eventual decision to marry Nina: 'Love Without Hope' and 'Death', in which the poet asks sorrowfully: 'Why must I love you/ When you will never be mine?/ I will never caress you/ It will not be me, who, exhausted by our caresses/ Falls asleep at your side' and, in the last song, seems to bid farewell to life: 'I am dying/ Without knowing love/ She did not love me/ She did not wait eagerly for me/ When I went away/ I am dying/ Because I cannot live without love.' The *Romances* are inescapably tragic, a final cry of pain from a man who had lost the woman he had loved for nearly ten years. There was no turning the clock back now: Tatiana was lost to him, and he had to find a way to move on. By the time he was orchestrating the songs, Shostakovich and Nina were married.

2

On the Edge of the Whirlwind

Shostakovich's opera *The Lady Macbeth of Mtsensk District* would acquire one of the most lurid reputations in the history of twentieth-century opera. Turning decisively away from the farce of *The Nose*, Shostakovich decided that an opera based on Nikolay Leskov's 1865 novella *Lady Macbeth* would be the first of a planned tetralogy of operas devoted to women. *Lady Macbeth* would show the degradation and despair of women living in the Tsarist era; the second opera was to have featured the women of the revolutionary movement 'People's Will' (*Narodnaya Volya*) and the third and fourth were to have celebrated different Soviet real-life heroines. Only *Lady Macbeth* was ever completed, because events over the next few years would put a stop to Shostakovich's career in opera; but at least initially, critical response to his opera was nothing short of rapturous. *Lady Macbeth* was staged not just in Leningrad's Maly Theatre, but simultaneously in Moscow's Nemirovich-Danchenko Theatre and later (from December 1934) at the Moscow Bolshoy's Filial Theatre as well. That the old team of Samuil Samosud and Nikolay Smolich at the Maly would have supported Shostakovich's second opera was gratifying, but not surprising: they had always believed in Shostakovich's operatic talent. But to have the Maly, Moscow's prestigious Nemirovich-Danchenko Theatre and the Bolshoy Filial all running simultaneous productions and vying for audiences to see this extraordinary new Soviet opera was completely unprecedented.

If operatic stature is measured in long production runs and international prestige, until *Lady Macbeth* there had not been any truly successful Soviet operas. Moscow and Leningrad theatre schedules were packed with old favourites like Saint-Saëns' *Samson and Delilah*, Verdi's *Rigoletto* and Tchaikovsky's *Eugene Onegin*. Various composers had written operas on Soviet themes (*For Red Petrograd* by Arseny Gladkovsky and *The Eagles' Revolt* by Andrey Pashchenko, both staged in 1925) but there had been nothing like the mature brilliance of *Lady Macbeth*. The Leningrad production opened on 22 January 1934, Nemirovich-Danchenko's (using the alternative title *Katerina Izmailova*) two days later. Until the productions were abruptly closed down in January 1936, they were wildly popular, with the Maly staging alone recording an average of 92.8 per cent capacity over the course of 1934 (49 performances in all).[1] As with the explosive success of his First Symphony, Shostakovich's opera would not just be a domestic hit. Over the next three years *Lady Macbeth* was performed in the United States, South America, Europe and Britain – not always fully staged, and not always to the levels of acclaim it had at home – but it spread Shostakovich's name worldwide, making him easily the most famous of Soviet composers and one of Soviet Russia's most successful musical exports.

The popularity of *Lady Macbeth* was clear: Shostakovich was sure of it, so were the directors of three major Russian opera theatres, so were his fellow composers and music critics, and so were the audiences who flocked to see it. But why should this opera have been such a hit when *The Nose* had not lasted more than a single season? There are two major reasons. First, Shostakovich had moved decisively away from the avant-garde language he had been addicted to since 1926. The shift had, in truth, already happened in the *Six Japanese Romances* and would be cemented further in his Cello Sonata of 1934. Now drawing deeply on the mastery of music-hall, operetta and dance styles he had acquired in his years of composing for theatre and ballet, Shostakovich brought the full armoury of his mature technique, from classical to popular, to bear on his new opera. The sheer breadth of its stylistic range was dazzling: Act One featured an agonized and terrifying passacaglia, a stately baroque form constructed over a repeated bass theme; but audiences also heard the sarcasm of the operetta waltz accompanying the ludicrous romantic plotting of the villainous father-in-law Boris Timofeyevich; they heard the sham grand opera style of the opera's main baddie Sergey as he seduces Katerina and later Sonyetka; they also heard the extreme violence of Shostakovich's now-familiar chase music style in the two shocking rape scenes of Act One. *Lady Macbeth* showed full-blown tragedy as well as comedy, and deep compassion as well as violence and mockery. After witnessing two sexual assaults, one savage beating, three murders and a suicide, the audience's gaze switches abruptly from Katerina's personal tragedy and suicide to a panorama of human misery in the shape of a convict transportation camp in Siberia.

That dramatic panning-out from personal suffering to collective pain comes as a powerful jolt at the end of an opera that has focused so intensely on its heroine. It is part of the second major reason for the opera's popularity and gives *Lady Macbeth* – the opera itself, not the character – a humanity that, some would argue, is missing from what has preceded it. For *Lady Macbeth*'s message was undeniably ideological, and Shostakovich himself made his intentions very plain in press statements and essays accompanying the premiere. Nikolay Leskov's original heroine Katerina had been unashamedly vicious and greedy, murdering her elderly father-in-law, husband and eight-year-old nephew in order to give her access not only to Sergey but to the Izmailovs' estate and business interests. Even at the very moment of her death by drowning (a horrifying murder-suicide in which Sergey's new lover Sonyetka is herself drowned by Katerina), Leskov makes it clear that it is Katerina, the 'huge pike' launching herself at the 'soft little perch' Sonyetka, who is the guilty party. Leskov set out to create a literary monster; Shostakovich sought to rehabilitate her in Soviet form. Collaborating with his librettist Alexander Preis, Shostakovich removed the nephew's murder, made the father-in-law into a violent, lustful bully and transformed the brutal Katerina into, as he put it, 'an intelligent, talented and interesting woman who, because of the nightmarish and harsh conditions in which she spends her life, and because of the cruel, venal environment of the merchant class, finds her existence bitter, dreary and miserable.'[2]

No wonder, then, that *Lady Macbeth* went down so well with Soviet audiences: it painted pre-revolutionary Russia as 'nightmarish', savaged the old merchant class as loathsome and corrupt, showed the degradation and assault of women as a fact of everyday life and revealed the horrible conditions of Tsarist prison transports across Siberia. In their deliberate deconstruction of Leskov, Shostakovich and Preis made their political point with all the subtlety of an agitprop poster, and it went something like this: Leskov could not see past Katerina's circumstances, which made her what she was; we, Soviet citizens, see that her behaviour was the inevitable result of Tsarist conditions. He condemned, while we, with our superior historical perspective, understand and thus exonerate. As a result, the opera is practically a whistle-stop tour of Soviet values in the late 1920s and early '30s: policemen and priests alike are ridiculed as corrupt drunks and members of the merchant class are seen as sub-humans leeching off the workers. Sergey, Katerina's lover, was described by Shostakovich in his booklet essay as a 'kulak' – a so-called 'rich peasant'. 'Kulak' was the revolting name given to peasants who during Stalin's First Five-year Plan (1928–32) were robbed, starved, arrested, exiled and murdered in the process of forced collectivization of the countryside, mostly unbeknown to residents in the major urban areas. As each social category is introduced, condemned and dispatched, Shostakovich's

Soviet audiences understood the political satire perfectly: precisely those images and messages had been directed at them since October 1917. By now those values had become so thoroughly normalized that the destruction of such characters had lost its power to shock.

What makes Shostakovich's Bolshevik reading of Leskov even more chilling is our knowledge of his next operatic plot. This has come to us through the memoirs of his friend Levon Atovmyan; recalled many years after discussing the opera with Shostakovich, doubtless some details are unreliable. But because it is not widely known (because the opera was never written), Atovmyan's plot summary bears (slightly abbreviated) reproduction here. This time the libretto was not based on a literary source: it was written by Alexander Preis on a plot of Shostakovich's own devising. The heroine, here called Sofia, is a member of the nineteenth-century terrorist organization 'The People's Will' (the real-life group who assassinated Tsar Alexander ii). The main characters are a General, an elderly official, his daughter Sofia and Vladimir, her lover. Both Sofia and Vladimir are members of the People's Will group.

Act One: A women's beach. Girls and women are shopping and walking around. Sounds of jolly, light-hearted song and conversation. Not far away, the General is sitting behind a bush and watching the girls on the beach through binoculars. His attention is caught by a beautiful blonde girl (Sofia).
Act Two: At the boulevard. The elderly official is walking with his daughter Sofia. Along comes the General, who recognizes Sofia as the girl he was watching on the beach. He invites them both to his home for tea. Once he has left them, Vladimir comes up to Sofia. They sing a love duet, where they promise to be true to one another.
Act Three: At the General's home. A luxurious residence with many guests. Dances; various guests sing songs. The General

seizes the chance to confess his love to Sofia. She replies that she already has a friend and won't betray him. Sofia's father intervenes and says that if she refuses the General's offer then, the General will drive him from his work and victimize him. Sofia is forced to consent to the General. They become engaged. Act Four: the General's office. He receives a document about the terrorist acts of the People's Will, whereupon the General flies into a rage, abuses his workers and declares that he himself will annihilate 'this plague', but he discovers that his own wife is part of the group, and thus this 'plague' is within his own house. Act Five: Returning home late, the General finds several people there, apparently Sofia's guests, Vladimir among them. Furious, the General says Sofia must leave the town and go to the General's country estate. Act Six: On the General's estate, amid scenes of country life. Sofia has not ceased her activities. Near the house a group of People's Will activists have gathered, among them Sofia and Vladimir. The General's carriage is expected – they all gather to meet it. They decide to throw a bomb at the carriage. Fate decrees that it will be Vladimir who throws the bomb. The General gets out of his carriage and sets off towards the house. Vladimir hesitates: does he have the right to kill Sofia's husband? Sofia runs up to Vladimir, takes the bomb from him and bravely approaches the General, throwing the bomb at him. It blows up and kills him, but it also fatally injures Sofia. The opera ends with an aria and chorus.[3]

The key word here is 'bravely'. If we accept Atovmyan's memory of the plot as reliable as to Shostakovich's fundamental intention – even if not every detail can be accurate – then, like Katerina's repulsive father-in-law Boris Timofeyevich in *Lady Macbeth*, the General deserves only to die. The dehumanizing technique used by Shostakovich and Preis is identical to that in *Lady Macbeth*: like

Boris Timofeyevich, the General is made ridiculous by presuming to lust after a beautiful young woman, who already has a lover her own age. His outbursts of anger and authority merely serve to underline his negative character. Sofia, the beautiful blonde, shows compassion to her own father but ruthlessly carries out the destruction of her hated husband, and in that final act is immortalized as a truly Soviet heroine-in-waiting. Could this gruesome scenario really have come from a composer who listed Anton Chekhov and Fëodor Dostoevsky among his favourite authors? Un-nuanced to the point of caricature, acts of extreme violence condoned and even celebrated, Shostakovich's plot for the second in his operatic trilogy is every bit the ideological equal of his reworking of Leskov's monstrous Katerina.

Yet if we are to understand why the Chekhov- and Dostoevsky-loving Shostakovich could have conceived such merciless plots, we must look beyond our own instinctive distaste and try to penetrate the composer's values and social conditioning. What seems inhumane today did not necessarily seem so to Shostakovich in 1934; rather, the true inhumanity in his mind lay in the social structures of Tsarist Russia, where even the abolition of serfdom in 1861 did not really emancipate the peasants (as with the abolition of slavery in Britain, it was the serf-owners who received generous government payouts, while the peasants themselves were left in some cases more impoverished than they had been before); where completely innocent citizens could be sent into 'administrative exile' in Siberia (a living death for many and a literal death for many more); where the vast structural and economic inequalities across the Russian Empire remained the lowest of low priorities for successive Tsars, and where exploitation, violence, early death and lack of basic care, education and rights were all considered absolutely normal. It is instructive to remind ourselves of some of the requests made in the 1905 petition to the Tsar that resulted in the 'Bloody Sunday' massacre in St Petersburg: freedom of the press and freedom to practise one's own religion; state education for all; an eight-hour working day and restrictions on overtime; equality of all before the law. The Russian working man and woman simply did not have these most basic of human and civil rights. Moreover, the organization 'People's Will' was not so far back in Russian history as all that: former members were still alive in Shostakovich's lifetime and regarded as heroes and heroines. The most famous of them was probably Vera Figner, a close personal friend of Sofia Perovskaya, Alexander II's assassin. She had been incarcerated in solitary confinement first in the Peter and Paul Fortress, St Petersburg, and then in the Schlüsselburg Fortress for twenty years, being finally released in 1904. She returned to Bolshevik Russia in 1917 from Europe and, though never joining the Communist Party officially, worked steadily for various good causes (when she died, aged ninety, in 1942 she was given a State funeral at the Novodevichy Cemetery in Moscow). Therefore the planned heroine of Shostakovich's 'People's Will' opera was not simply an invented class murderer in the Stalinist mould; she was based on a model of female martyrdom then regarded as the epitome of nobility and self-sacrifice (and anyone reading Figner's memoirs even today, though likely to be struck by her commitment to violence, could not help but be impressed by her loyalty to her principles).[4] It is also instructive to recall that Shostakovich's educated, liberal parents were, like many of that social class, supporters of at least the February Revolution of 1917 and had on occasion both supported and interceded for victims of the Tsarist regime prior to 1917, including those sent to Siberia or other prisons. Looking backwards at Shostakovich's career from the vantage point of 1934, it seems that Shostakovich took that support and extended it to the point where he willingly constructed some of his greatest music around what strikes us now as the crudest Bolshevik propaganda – and, what is more, did so during the years of Stalin's notorious First Five-year Plan.

It is temptingly easy to apply hindsight to Shostakovich's career and conclude that, because we associate Stalinism with political terror and the cult of personality, the most humane and intelligent among Soviet citizens must have viewed Stalin as evil from the start. Yet when dealing with this period of Russian history, chronology is everything, and political changes could come with bewildering speed. Stalin's Soviet Union of purges and repressions (the Great Terror spanned approximately 1936–9) was, at least to those dwelling in major cities (that is, those unaffected by collectivization), a very different place to that between 1932–5 and few, if any, could have foreseen what the writer Evgenia Ginzburg aptly termed the 'whirlwind' of political terror to come.[5] To immortalize early revolutionary values in the early Stalin years, then, is not necessarily 'Stalinist' as we would understand it now. Yet it might also be wise to remember that, just before starting work on *Lady Macbeth*, Shostakovich had already seen friends and family associates arrested, so it was not the case that he was a political naïf either. His classmate at the Conservatoire, Alexander Kenel, was arrested in 1927 in connection with his membership of the sect 'Knights of the Grail' and sentenced to three years in the Solovetsky camps. His old friend Mikhail Kvadri, dedicatee of the First Symphony, was arrested and shot in 1929. Shostakovich's godfather, Pëtr Polevoy, was arrested in 1930 and given ten years for alleged spying (he went to a camp in Vorkuta, but after intercession from the President of the Academy of Sciences was freed after seven years). The priest who baptized Shostakovich and who remained a family friend was arrested in 1931 and sent to work on the White Sea canal (released after two years). As Shostakovich and Preis were formulating the scenario for their 'People's Will' opera, yet more arrests would have come to the composer's attention: an acquaintance of Shostakovich's youth, the painter Solomon Gershov, was arrested in Leningrad in April 1932 and all his work destroyed. And even more personally distressing, the composer

Boleslav Yavorsky, theorist and pedagogue.

and partner of Shostakovich's good friend Boleslav Yavorsky, Vladimir Protopopov, was arrested in 1934 and sentenced to two years penal labour.[6]

In short, Shostakovich at the point of working on both *Lady Macbeth* and *Narodnaya Volya* was well acquainted with the Soviet justice system, the machinations of the OGPU (the forerunner of the NKVD, itself the forerunner of the KGB), and the dangers of being arrested – even shot – when completely innocent of any real crime. But though we have these facts at our disposal, we do not know how Shostakovich reacted to them. At this stage intercession could still bring people back from Siberia or free them from prison: both Shostakovich himself and his family got involved in such cases in the 1930s, and Shostakovich would intervene on behalf of arrested friends and colleagues for the rest of the Stalin era and even beyond. There is only one thing we can be reasonably sure about with regard to Shostakovich's political/creative calculations at this time, and that is that the ideological messages of both operas seemed, at least to Shostakovich and Preis, entirely in keeping with the mood of the times. If Shostakovich did fear arrest, it would not have been over the plot of *Lady Macbeth*; rather, he had good reason to believe that the opera's political credentials could only have reflected well upon him.

Amid the tumultuous success of *Lady Macbeth*, Shostakovich's recent marriage was, as might have been expected, getting off to a rocky start. Relations were not helped by animosity between Nina's family and Shostakovich's mother Sofia who, according to his sister Maria, had felt snubbed when she first went to visit Nina's parents and never really warmed to her daughter-in-law. Initially Nina moved into the Shostakovich family apartment, still a *kommunalka* on Marat Street, near Leningrad's Moscow Station. Just over a year later Shostakovich bought a small three-room apartment through a housing co-operative on nearby Dmitrovsky Lane for himself and Nina, but also for his mother, who remained in that apartment for the rest of her life. Shostakovich and Nina would not move out into their own private apartment until a little later, when the recently founded House of Composers in Leningrad found them a more permanent residence on Vasilevsky Island. It was not the easiest of beginnings to any marriage, though far from untypical in those years. But between the early summer of 1934 and October 1935 Shostakovich was by no means sure that he wished to remain married to Nina after all. During the International Music Festival in Leningrad in May 1934, he met a young translator named Yelena Konstantinovskaya and fell deeply in love. His love letters to her, only snippets of which have ever been made available, show that she had become the new focus of Shostakovich's most passionate feelings. While touring in the Black Sea in the summer of 1934, he wrote to her adoringly:

As for love, you shouldn't be angry about it. I can't do
anything about myself. I'm trying to stop loving you,
to finish it, but instead I love you more and more. And
there is a lot of sadness and grief in my love . . .
It's likely that this letter is the last. I can't describe how sad
and upset I am. Can it be that you'll disappear completely from
my life after turning up by chance? I dread the thought . . .
I'm leaving on 12 August. It's always very scary to come
back home after a long absence. You always seem to
come across some misfortune or other. I must confess
that I've been trying to stop loving you all this time, but
nothing came out of it. I'm dreaming of you falling in
love with me and becoming my wife. See how much I'm
dreaming, despite the fact that I'm sort of married.[7]

After this summer of pining, it is not surprising that
Shostakovich and Nina separated, at Nina's insistence. When the
couple moved back to Leningrad in the autumn, they tried again
to make their marriage work, but by early 1935 Shostakovich was
again seen in public openly with Konstantinovskaya and wrote to
Sollertinsky that he might move permanently to Moscow with his
mother, leaving Nina in the Dmitrovsky apartment.[8]

Shostakovich and Nina formally divorced in early 1935, but
they began seeing each other again that summer, and by October
they were remarried. Sollertinsky, Shostakovich's close confidant
through all these troubles, received a brief update in a postscript
in a letter dated 30–31 October 1935: 'There is to be no more
talk of my divorce from Nina. I have only now come to realize
what an amazing woman she is, and how dear to me.'[9] Another
of Shostakovich's friends from those years, Abram Ashkenazy,
would later shed further light on this whole episode. He reported
that Nina suffered from nephritis, a kidney disease that, in those
days, meant that doctors informed women they would die in

childbirth. Shostakovich, who dearly wanted children, was terribly upset by this and Nina's diagnosis coincided with his affair with Konstantinovskaya (who was actually denounced, arrested and imprisoned in 1935, though released in early 1936). Nina received treatment and became pregnant in September 1935 after their summer of reunion; it was after this that they remarried. Once Shostakovich became a father, there would be no more serious dalliances on his side (though he certainly did continue to fall in love with other women and very probably had affairs with several of them). But though his family life was stable, and though no one who knew him questioned his devotion to his wife, their marriage would never be entirely normal by most people's standards. Nina, a professional scientist, formed a relationship with her old classmate, the physicist Artëm Alikhanyan, and after the war began spending

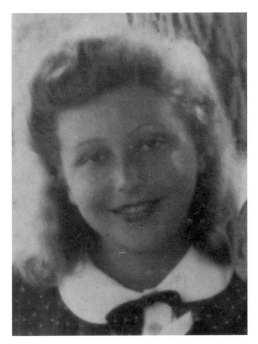

Yelena
Konstantinovskaya,
Shostakovich's
girlfriend in 1934.

a part of each year with him in Yerevan working in his laboratory. Ashkenazy recalled that when Nina and Alikhanyan first began their relationship, which he says was before the outbreak of war, Shostakovich said to her, 'Do as you please, we are both free.'[10] And so the Shostakovich marriage proceeded along these unorthodox lines, with Nina's secondary relationship openly acknowledged. It did not prevent their marriage from being in many ways a strong one, and Shostakovich would be devastated by his wife's early death in 1954. Nina, herself a formidable and highly intelligent woman, was the ideal foil for Shostakovich's contrary personality: though creatively steely, with absolute faith in his calling as a composer, he was unable to stand up for himself, sometimes in the simplest things. She would be his greatest friend and protector through the worst years of Stalinism to come.

Much has been written about the precise timings of the political purges, show trials and Shostakovich's personal fall from grace in January and February 1936. Certainly, until the moment Shostakovich read the editorial in *Pravda* on 28 January 1936 entitled 'Muddle Instead of Music' about his opera *Lady Macbeth*, he had no reason to fear for either his career or his personal safety. That editorial changed everything. Overnight Shostakovich was transformed from the Soviet Union's most fêted composer to someone whose name could hardly be mentioned without reference to his crimes against the art of music. *Lady Macbeth* was immediately taken off the stage and the 'decadent' Western modernist repertoire that had supposedly corrupted Shostakovich's style was wiped from concert programmes. The recently formed Composers' Union, finding itself called to account for the failings of its most successful member, called meetings in Leningrad and Moscow to discuss the 'problems' of Soviet music. Sollertinsky, recognized by everyone as a major influence on Shostakovich, was forced to accept part of the blame for Shostakovich's descent into Western-inspired decadence. From being Shostakovich's

'Muddle Instead of Music', *Pravda*, 28 January 1936.

most ardent supporter, Sollertinsky (with Shostakovich's private permission and blessing) admitted that the opera he himself had formerly praised was, indeed, full of 'formalism' and incomprehensible to the Soviet listener. The entire Leningrad Composers' Union voted in favour of the *Pravda* editorial, with just one exception: the composer Vladimir Shcherbachëv, who abstained.[11]

Though for a long time there were rumours that Stalin himself had written 'Muddle Instead of Music', we now know that it was written by the party official David Zaslavsky, at Stalin's personal instigation. Having been to hear *Lady Macbeth*, Stalin was evidently appalled to realize that this famous opera, sent all over the world as a major achievement of Soviet culture, was not the kind of music he liked at all. Known to love attending Tchaikovsky operas at the Bolshoy, and in general conservative in his cultural tastes, Stalin had been impressed by the last Soviet opera he had been to see: Ivan Dzerzhinsky's feeble (and very selective) setting of Mikhail Sholokhov's great novel *The Quiet Don*. *Lady Macbeth* was in a different league in every respect, though, like Dzerzhinsky, Shostakovich had believed his opera to be ideologically respectable. It transpired, however, that there was ideology not just in an opera's message but in its very musical fabric. *Lady Macbeth* was judged to have been corrupted by Western influences, its language 'chaotic' and 'confused'. *Pravda*'s editorial ranted: 'To follow this "music" is difficult; to remember it is impossible . . . singing . . . is replaced by shrieking.' Even the ideological message of the opera was mocked: 'He [Shostakovich] portrays the merchants and the people monotonously and bestially. The predatory merchant woman who scrambles into the possession of wealth through murder is pictured as some kind of "victim" of bourgeois society.'[12] The musical illiteracy of 'Muddle Instead of Music', which inaccurately accused Shostakovich of using jazz to spice up his language, even provoked the writer Maxim Gorky to come to Shostakovich's defence. Using his privileged position as defender of the art world with a hotline to Stalin, Gorky wrote scornfully of the editorial's clumsiness:

> The article in *Pravda* has fallen like a ton of bricks on his head, the lad is completely dejected . . . How and where is this 'muddle' expressed? The critics have an obligation to give a technically precise definition of Shostakovich's music. The only thing that the *Pravda* article has done is to provoke herds of ungifted people and all kinds of charlatans to hound Shostakovich.[13]

This astonishing letter to Stalin had no discernible effect and nor, evidently, did the letter that Shostakovich's powerful political friend, Marshal Mikhail Tukhachevsky, wrote to Stalin. In fact, Tukhachevsky's brave letter (Shostakovich told his friend

Isaak Glikman that beads of sweat ran down his face as he was writing it), which revealed the friendship between the Marshal and Shostakovich to Stalin, may have put Shostakovich in an even more dangerous position when the following year Tukhachevsky found himself facing a far more lethal charge than composing decadent music.[14] Shostakovich appealed not only to his most powerful friend, but to the Head of the Committee on Arts Affairs, Platon Kerzhentsev. Both made it clear to him that the statements made about *Lady Macbeth* could not be retracted, and that the only option available was to confess the error of his ways and promise to reform. Shostakovich accepted the advice and carried on working. But the symphony that followed, of which two movements of the three were already finished before 'Muddle Instead of Music' was published, showed no sign that the composer was prepared to compromise when it came to his own music. As Shostakovich remarked to Glikman, reminiscing in 1974 about this period, 'the authorities tried everything they knew to get me to repent and expiate my sin. But I refused. I was young then, and had my strength. Instead of repenting, I composed the Fourth Symphony.'[15]

By April Shostakovich had completed his new work and Fritz Stiedry, then chief conductor of the Leningrad Philharmonia, scheduled its premiere for December 1936. By May Shostakovich had become a father, with the birth of his daughter Galina. That autumn Stiedry began rehearsing the symphony and, as the premiere date approached, the orchestra and its management team grew increasingly anxious. There are conflicting stories about why, in the end, the Fourth Symphony was not performed. According to Glikman, it was the director of the Philharmonia, the pianist Isay Renzin, who advised Shostakovich to withdraw it, so as not to attract yet more criticism and perhaps lead not only himself, but the orchestra as well, into serious trouble. Stiedry himself remembered that the orchestra began to sabotage the rehearsal once they had begun on the finale, deliberately refusing to play properly; and Shostakovich reportedly told the younger composer Rodion Shchedrin that the orchestra had actually mounted a vociferous complaint.[16] Shostakovich withdrew his Fourth Symphony from rehearsal in December. It would not be played again for 25 years.

What was it about this symphony that so upset the orchestra? Specifically, what was it about the finale? It opened with the same kind of homage to Gustav Mahler that had already been plain in the second movement, which was a kind of Soviet reworking of the folky Austrian *Ländler* beloved of both Mahler and Anton Bruckner, and familiar to Leningrad audiences. This time the Mahler connection was a spare, quietly paced funeral march, a little like that of the 'Frère Jacques' funeral march of Mahler's First Symphony. Presumably there was nothing in that to cause unrest. But the slow march unravels and begins to spiral out of control, rushing headlong into a raging, stamping transformation of a waltz that, at its climax, comes very close to a direct quotation from *Lady Macbeth* (just before figure 187). Thereafter follows a sequence of circus-like miniatures, which, as the Shostakovich scholar Olga Digonskaya has revealed, came straight from the shelved *People's Will* opera.[17] Touching, comical and grotesque by turns, the sequence was brilliant, if disorientating for a symphonic finale. But perhaps it was the ending that alarmed the orchestra most of all. The sequence dies away, alluding to the 'Resurrection' theme from Mahler's Second Symphony as all that had gone before is swept away into near-silence. Then, bursting in like a heavy military parade grinding all before it into the dust, comes the terrifying return of the funeral march: all-consuming, pitiless, a raging destructive force. As suddenly as it had come, the march is abruptly sucked away, leaving in its wake a shell-shocked emptiness. Numbed and traumatized, fragments of the funeral march turn in on themselves. Pinpricks of sound on celeste evoke the dying of the light. Now soft to the point of inaudible, the symphony closes in an atmosphere of impenetrable darkness.

To understand the orchestra's fear, we have to try and grasp just how dangerous it could have been to perform such music. The age of modernist experimentation in the Soviet Union was long since over: a symphony was a public statement of mass sentiment, ideally of a rousing, collective kind. Symphonies of this type had already become common practice: those by Nikolay Myaskovsky provide particularly good points of comparison, especially his Twelfth, written during 1931–2. The overarching theme of that symphony, which sought to depict the joy of work in a collective farm, provides the starkest possible comparison with Shostakovich's Fourth. One was all sunlight and smiling Soviet peasants: the musical equivalent of the painter Arkady Plastov's *Collective Farm Celebration* or Sergey Gerasimov's *Collective Farm Harvest Festival*, both dating from 1937. The other showed Stalin's Soviet Union as a place of violence and horror. Socialist realism, the aesthetic principle expected of all artists since 1934, demanded that works of art be accessible and 'party-minded' in guiding Soviet citizens to look at all times towards a brighter future. Myaskovsky's symphony clearly fulfilled those expectations; Shostakovich's, just as clearly, did not.

The year 1936 proved a turning point for Shostakovich. By the end of that year he knew what it felt like to be denounced by friends and colleagues; he had seen his greatest work sent into oblivion and feared for the survival of those dear to him – which is why he gave Sollertinsky carte blanche to say anything that would save him from further punishment – and had seen the climate of fear beginning to shroud the whole country. Though historians commonly date the 'Great Terror' from 1936, political purges of the Communist Party's membership began even earlier: the assassination of the Leningrad Party leader Sergey Kirov in December 1934 launched the first wave of expulsions and arrests and coincided so tidily with Stalin's removal of potential rivals within the Politburo that some historians have surmised that Kirov's murder was arranged by Stalin himself. This has certainly never been proven, but what we do know is that immediately after Kirov's murder two Old Bolsheviks, Lev Kamenev and Grigory Zinoviev, together with their closest colleagues, were arrested, tried in January 1935 and sentenced to ten-year prison terms. In August 1936 Kamenev, Zinoviev and fourteen other Old Bolsheviks were hauled out of prison and put on trial again in what would become the first of three infamous Moscow show trials. Kamenev and Zinoviev were taken from the courtroom and shot, and their executions were celebrated in the Soviet press. Over the next two years Stalin would exterminate nearly all his former Party colleagues, some dragged before the courts in show trials, others arrested and tried behind closed doors before their execution. As the purges swept the Party through 1935 to 1938, they extended their reach, initially to the Red Army and eventually to all walks of life, with quotas set for arrests per district.

But if Shostakovich would never be quite the same person again after 1936, there was worse to follow, both for himself and his fellow citizens, since 1937 saw a significant ratcheting up of political terror, and by now ordinary people – not just politicians or the military – were living in fear of arrest. One of the first victims well known to Shostakovich was his powerful friend and protector Marshal Mikhail Tukhachevsky, whose tragic fate engulfed all those closest to him. Tukhachevsky was very good friends with the Moscow composer and musicologist Nikolay Zhilayev, who held musical gatherings at his home, to which Shostakovich and Tukhachevsky would occasionally go. Zhilayev was not only a deeply respected musician, but was dearly loved by his colleagues and students, not only for his vast erudition but for his conspicuous generosity and care towards his fellow musicians. He had particular affection for Shostakovich, whose talent he venerated. In May 1937 Shostakovich played the second movement of his Fifth Symphony to Zhilayev in one of his social evenings. The composer Grigory Fried recalled that, after hearing Shostakovich perform, Zhilayev patted Shostakovich on the head 'with paternal tenderness, repeating almost inaudibly "Mitya, Mitya."' After Shostakovich had left, Zhilayev whispered in awe, 'Mitya is a genius, a genius.'[18] This distinguished musician, whom Shostakovich held in deep respect, would suffer the ultimate punishment for his friendship with Tukhachevsky. Days after this friendly gathering, on 22 May 1937, Tukhachevsky was arrested in connection with an alleged plot to assassinate Stalin.

Thereafter a whole catalogue of tragedies unfolded around Shostakovich. On 5 June his mother wrote in desperation to the pianist Lev Nikolayev (Shostakovich's former Conservatoire teacher) about the 'great misfortune' that had befallen the Shostakovich family. Shostakovich's older sister Maria, to whom he was always closest, had been arrested and sentenced to exile in Central Asia (to Frunze, now Bishkek, Kyrgyzstan) after her husband, the scientist Vsevolod Frederiks, was taken away in the middle of the night and given a penal sentence (under what charge his wife never knew), leaving the elderly Sofia Shostakovich to care for their son, now left without either parent.[19] Then the Tukhachevsky noose began to tighten further. The Marshal was shot on 12 June and announced in the Soviet press to have been an 'enemy of the people'. In July that year Shostakovich's close friend Atovmyan was arrested. Then Zhilayev himself was arrested on 3 November and accused of plotting with Tukhachevsky to assassinate Stalin. The composer was shot on 20 January 1938. An appeal for clemency, dated 4 September 1940 and signed by Zhilayev's Conservatoire colleagues Alexander Goldenweiser, Nikolay Myaskovsky, Samuil Feinberg, Konstantin Igumnov, Reingold Glier, Alexander Alexandrov and Alexander Gedike, tragically reached Vyacheslav Molotov far too late to save Zhilayev, showing that none of his friends had any idea what had happened to him.[20] It must have seemed ludicrous to them that a Conservatoire professor, a former pupil of Sergey Taneyev and a mainstay of Moscow's musical elite, could possibly have been charged with anything at all. That he could actually have been shot must have seemed utterly unthinkable.

This imaginary plot to assassinate Stalin almost sucked Shostakovich himself into its vortex. The composer Veniamin Basner, a good friend of Shostakovich's, told the cellist Elizabeth Wilson that, in the spring of 1937, Shostakovich was summoned to the NKVD headquarters in Leningrad for an interview. He arrived at the prescribed time and, as the interview went on, Shostakovich realized that he was there because of Tukhachevsky. His interrogator probed as to the precise nature of their relationship before suddenly demanding, 'I think you should try and shake your memory . . . For instance, the plot to assassinate Comrade Stalin? What did you hear about that?' At that moment, Basner told Wilson, Shostakovich knew his fate was sealed. His interrogator gave him the weekend to burnish his faulty memory and instructed him to return on Monday. So far as Shostakovich knew, that would be the last he would ever see of Nina and their baby. After spending what he imagined would be their last few days together, Shostakovich returned for further interrogation, only to be turned away at the door. It seemed his interrogator had himself been arrested and there was no need for Shostakovich to be questioned.[21]

Given that Tukhachevsky was arrested on 22 May and shot on 12 June, this event must have taken place between those dates. Basner reported that, at the time of Shostakovich's interrogation, Tukhachevsky's fate, and the charge against him, was not yet known. Although it is clear that the NKVD had a list of names of those on friendly terms with the Marshal, and that Shostakovich was associated with him through Zhilayev, at the time of this interview Zhilayev himself had not been arrested, and would not be taken for several more months. But arrests were at that precise moment sweeping through Shostakovich's own family. We do not know if there was any connection between Tukhachevsky's arrest and that of Shostakovich's sister, brother-in-law and mother-in-law (Nina's mother was also arrested at this time). It is possible that the family was implicated in some way through Shostakovich's paternal uncle (by marriage) Maxim Kostrikin, who, along with nearly all his generation of Old Bolsheviks, was also arrested in 1937 and executed. In this horrific network of terror, literally every adult Soviet citizen could be implicated by a present or previous association with someone that had been deemed suspicious. Basner assumed that Shostakovich had not relayed this story to many people, but we really have no way of knowing whether that was true or not. The fact that he also told it to the Polish composer Krzysztof Meyer suggests that Shostakovich did tell others, perhaps more towards the end of his life. But it was not the kind of casual anecdote that could be passed on to all and sundry, especially not in the Stalin years themselves. Such a narrow escape, especially when so many others had fared infinitely worse, could not have been confided to any but a trusted few, but the fact that those few did not all commit the story to record, or apparently discuss it between themselves, does not mean they were never told.

Either way, it is fair to ask the question: how did Shostakovich survive, when he had attracted the disapproval of Stalin himself? There are several possible answers, and one has come to us in the form of a transcript of a discussion between Stalin, the Kremlin film expert Boris Shumiatsky and Stalin's Politburo colleagues Vyacheslav Molotov and Kliment Voroshilov on 29 January 1936, the day after 'Muddle Instead of Music' was published. The discussion ran as follows (summary only):

Voroshilov to Shumiatsky: What do you think of *Pravda*'s opinion of Shostakovich?
Shumiatsky: I completely agree with it. I have been calling for joyful, realistic music for years, and have written on this theme more than once . . .

Molotov: What about film music?

Shumiatsky: There are several decent symphonic and vocal melodies, for examples in *The Golden Mountains*, *The Storm*, *Aerograd*, *Jolly Fellows*, and some good examples of the best Soviet mass songs: 'The morning greets us', 'March of the jolly fellows' . . .

Stalin: 'The morning greets us' is from *Jolly Fellows*. In this film all the songs are good, simple and melodic . . .

Voroshilov: 'The morning greets us' – is this from *The Counterplan* by Shostakovich?

Shumiatsky: Yes, he wrote the song. I personally think Shostakovich is a great composer who can write good realistic music, but he needs guidance.

Stalin: That's just it. He has no one to guide him. People rush into these labyrinths of affectation . . . then when *Pravda* gives them elucidation, all our composers have to start creating music that is clear and comprehensible, not enigmatic, in which any sense of order perishes. And so it is necessary, so that people are able to use melodies. In some films, we are deafened. The orchestra crackles, squeals, pipes, jingles, disturbs your visual images. Why is leftism so tenacious in music? There is only one answer: no one keeps an eye on [composers] and composers and conductors don't address the demands of clear mass art.[22]

This revealing exchange tells us a number of things. It tells us clearly that when Stalin's official David Zaslavsky wrote 'Muddle Instead of Music', he had taken his cue very literally from Stalin himself: the description of music that 'crackles and squeals' quotes almost word for word from the *Pravda* editorial. It also tells us that Voroshilov and Shumiatsky may have saved Shostakovich's reputation with Stalin by pointing out that 'The morning greets us' was composed not for the film *Jolly Fellows*, but for the 1932 film *The Counterplan*. This song, which was known to all Soviet citizens with access to a radio, is generally known as 'The Song of the Counterplan' and was Shostakovich's first and only popular hit song. But though this intervention certainly did Shostakovich no harm, we will probably never know how it was that he survived when other Soviet artists perished, including many to whom he was close – above all the great theatre director Vsevolod Meyerhold, arrested in 1939 and, though this was not revealed until after Stalin's death, shot in prison in 1940. Shostakovich did survive, but his life, and his music, would never be the same again.

Alongside the Fourth Symphony, the work that speaks most eloquently of the terror years is the symphony that even today is Shostakovich's single most popular and well-known work: his Fifth. He had begun work on it about a year after completing the Fourth, making sketches of the whole in April 1937 and completing the first and second movements very quickly (recalling that he was able to perform the second movement to Zhilayev in May 1937). The slow movement, which Shostakovich claimed to have written down in just three days, was therefore conceived over the course of that fateful summer of 1937, exactly at the point when his family and friends began to be taken from him, and he put the finishing touches to his symphony on 20 September 1937. This time it was not Stiedry who would perform it: as a foreigner (in fact a refugee from Nazi Germany), Stiedry had not had his contract renewed and he was forced to leave the Soviet Union. The momentous responsibility of premiering Shostakovich's new symphony fell to a young conductor, Yevgeny Mravinsky. Later in life, Mravinsky recalled that he had not fully appreciated at the time just what a potentially dangerous undertaking this had been: it was the symphony that would make or break Shostakovich's reputation and the Leningrad Philharmonia itself could not afford to take any risks, as it was at that precise moment going through a purge of its administration and orchestra.[23] This time the orchestra had confidence in the new work, and the premiere went ahead on 21 November 1937. Eyewitness accounts of the occasion have passed into legend: the

Leningrad audience, emotionally battered and terrorized by the personal losses so many of them had suffered that year, began to weep during the slow movement. As the finale turned dramatically to the major right at the end, the audience began, one by one, to rise to their feet; Shostakovich was called out for ovation after ovation. Amid shouts of 'bravo', Mravinsky held Shostakovich's score high above his head. The artist Lyubov Yakovleva remembered that 'Everybody repeated the same phrase over and over again: "He's given his answer, and it was a good one." D. D. [Shostakovich] went out on stage as pale as can be, biting his lips. I thought he was about to burst into tears.'[24]

The idea of Shostakovich's 'answer' rapidly took root. An as-yet unidentified critic had remarked that the Fifth had been Shostakovich's 'creative answer of a Soviet artist to just criticism', and Shostakovich (perhaps guided by Sollertinsky, ever the master of media spin) published an article taking this idea ('My Creative Answer') as his title. As Laurel Fay has pointed out, however, there was nothing in the Fifth to suggest that Shostakovich had fundamentally altered his style.[25] It was an 'answer', but not an apology or a retraction. For the most part, the Fifth Symphony is as dark a work as the Fourth, perhaps even darker, given that the Fourth had no slow movement, and certainly nothing like the overt tragedy of its successor. But what it did have was a bombastic major-key ending: it concluded not with the dying of the light but in a blaze of glory.

So, had Shostakovich decided to follow Myaskovsky's example and show a 'party-minded' optimism in his finale? Some listeners even at the time found the turn to the major unconvincing. Myaskovsky himself noted in his diary, 'the ending is bad – the D major formal reply'.[26] The poet Osip Mandelshtam described it as 'tedious intimidation'.[27] And the heavyweight critic Georgy Khubov wrote disapprovingly that the ending feels like 'the embodiment of a superb but *external*, elemental, subjugating force . . . And that is why the general impression of this symphony's finale is not so much bright and optimistic as it is severe and threatening.'[28] Perhaps most memorably of all, the Soviet writer Alexander Fadeyev wrote in his diary that 'the ending does not sound like a resolution (still less feel like a triumph or victory), but rather like a punishment or vengeance on someone. A terrible emotional force, but a tragic force.'[29]

Yet the Leningrad audience had risen to their feet during the ending. What is going on in this finale to divide critical opinion so sharply? It is clear from the score that Shostakovich did deliberately set up the coda (the symphony's final section) as a kind of anti-coda. The finale contains two themes, one (the opening) in D minor, menacing and aggressive; the other, in a major key, which guides the listener towards the light. When we first hear it (fig. 108) it is battling against its violent neighbour, briefly erupting in triumph (fig. 110). At this moment the bright theme has an epic, filmic quality, making it a real moment of breakthrough. But the return of the opening theme quickly closes it down; and this gives way to its third iteration, now on solo horn (fig. 112) in a passage that gives us the first real moment of beauty and rest. Following a brief, anguished transformation, the finale then turns to quotation to make its point crystal-clear. At fig. 120 Shostakovich quotes from his own song, 'Rebirth', from his *Four Romances on Texts of A. Pushkin*, which he had recently completed and orchestrated. The rocking figure we hear on first violins and harp in the symphony is copied straight from the song 'Rebirth', instantly bringing to mind, for anyone knowing it, its highly suggestive text:

An artist-barbarian, with careless brush
Blackens a picture of genius.
And his sinful drawing
Scrawls meaninglessly over it.
But over the years, that alien paint
Flakes off like old scales.

The work of genius returns to us
In its former beauty.
Thus delusions fall
From my tormented soul.
And from within again spring up
Visions of former, pure days.

Wreathed in beauty, the Pushkin quotation is intimately connected with the major-key theme in its last guise: they share the same gentle orchestration, even the same (or very similar) rocking figure on violins. The key, too, is the same (B flat major). The vision ends and, at first slowly, the dark minor-key theme reasserts itself before we are propelled inexorably to the noisy triumph of the D-major ending. If it sounds like a hollow victory, it was supposed to. By showing us the real beauty – giving us that privileged glimpse into the inner sanctum – Shostakovich exposes the coda's fakery. Those critics who disliked the bombast had listened with the sharpest ears of all; and yet we cannot discount the Leningraders' cheers. I would like to suggest here that the Leningrad response was, at least in part, shaped by a huge wave of relief, even catharsis. And I believe it is also true that Shostakovich did not insult his audiences by giving them a finale that did not musically succeed: in a fine performance, the coda *is* effective, even uplifting. But at the same time, Shostakovich laid an ingenious musical trail that told a quite different story. The strategy was both brilliant and courageous, and it worked. It was Shostakovich's Fifth Symphony, not Myaskovsky's Twelfth, or even his far more successful Sixteenth (premiered and warmly received in October 1936), that Soviet orchestras programmed year after year. Whether Shostakovich's foes liked it or not, he had created a masterpiece – and everyone knew it.

3

Civic Responsibility and Self-assertion

After the immense emotional stress of 1937 and the success of his Fifth Symphony, Shostakovich experienced a lull in his creative powers that lasted almost a whole year. Clearly feeling that he had reached a turning point in his career, he took the surprising step of once again approaching his old mentor Boleslav Yavorsky for lessons. On 31 May 1938 he wrote:

> After much deliberation and embarrassment over the last four years I have come to the decision to return to you with a huge request: to take me as your student. I know all the musicians in Moscow and Leningrad very well and on my considered reflection I decided to repeat the request that I put to you in 1925–1926. Back then it was circumstances that put paid to my great desire to study with the great musician Boleslav Yavorsky. Now my circumstances are to some degree successful.[1]

Shostakovich suggested that they could meet once every six weeks or so. Following his son Maxim's birth that summer, he repeated his request, writing again on 26 July 1938:

> I would like to enrol with you as a student (and I don't use that term coquettishly, but in complete seriousness) and I consider it essential to fully acquaint you with my latest works: that is, the Five Fragments (1935), the Fourth Symphony (1935–1936) and

Four Romances on Texts by Pushkin (1936). Apart from those, I am now writing a quartet. I have composed two movements. None of these works are published or performed yet. It is essential for you to know these works to get the complete picture.[2]

We have no record of Yavorsky's reply, but we might guess that he persuaded Shostakovich that any such lessons would not provide the reassurance and change of direction he was groping for. So far as we know, the lessons never took place, though their friendship would endure until Yavorsky's tragically early death during the war in 1941.

When he finally began composing again in the summer of 1938 Shostakovich turned to a completely new genre. Perhaps inspired by Vissarion Shebalin's Second Quartet from 1935 with its passacaglia slow movement, Shostakovich sought his new path not only in the quartet genre, but in its classical influence. Shebalin and Shostakovich were lifelong friends – always Mitya and Ronya to each other – and in 1944 Shostakovich would dedicate his own Second Quartet to him. However, the First Quartet was not actually Shostakovich's first experience of composing for that medium: in 1934–5 he had composed a strikingly original score for his friend Lev Arnshtam's film *Girlfriends* (*Podrugi*, released 1936). In every respect a classical art-house film, *Girlfriends* opens with what became the slow movement of the Quartet. Shostakovich's music is present, even foregrounded, for so much of the film that Stalin, during one of his Kremlin screenings, apparently complained that it spoiled his enjoyment of the plot: 'There's far too much music. It interferes with our perception.'[3] From the first view of the village from whence spring the three little girls on whose friendship the film is based, we hear Shostakovich's gritty string quartet scoring accompanying everyday events, even the girls' conversation, with no attempt at more familiar diegetic scoring until much later (including the girls' singing of the revolutionary song 'Tormented by Grievous Bondage' in a workers' bar).

Though we often think of Shostakovich's film scores as inhabiting a world quite separate from his 'serious' music, probably because we know he found writing for the propaganda potboilers of the late 1940s unrewarding, in fact there was often cross-pollination between his film music and other works. The experience of writing for string quartet in *Girlfriends* clearly acted as an effective trial run for the first of what would be one of the most substantial bodies of quartet writing of the last century. And though the film itself is certainly propagandistic, it is not crassly so; Arnshtam was a talented director, as were all those with whom Shostakovich worked, and most of them were also personal friends. That Arnshtam welcomed such a tough score for his first major film speaks volumes about his faith in Shostakovich's music; by the time the film was released, the relatively open culture of 1934–5 had turned decisively in a far more repressive direction and Shostakovich's name was no longer a selling point for a new film. Owing to Stalin's personal involvement with the Soviet film industry, many distinguished directors and screenwriters met tragic fates in the purge years, including one of the screenwriters of *Girlfriends*, Raisa Vasileva, who died in the Gulag in 1938. Yet despite Stalin's dislike of the music, the film was well received and no more adverse criticism was directed at Shostakovich, even if this radical approach to film scoring would not be repeated in future collaborations.

Though the opening music of *Podrugi* serves as the First Quartet's slow movement, it opens with music far more genial: Shostakovich himself announced in the paper *Izvestiya* that his new work was 'joyful, merry, lyrical . . . spring-like'.[4] And this marked the start of a series of relatively sunny works that, taken as a group, contrast sharply not only with the Fourth and Fifth Symphonies that precede them, but, more surprisingly, with events unfolding around Shostakovich in the years 1938–40. Although the purges of his family circle had stopped, many more artists from Leningrad and Moscow's elite circles continued to disappear. Persecution of Shostakovich's older friend and faithful supporter Vsevolod Meyerhold began in January 1938 with the closure of his Moscow Art Theatre; in May the poet Osip Mandelshtam, who had read an insulting poem about Stalin to a circle of people he assumed to be close friends, was denounced and arrested. The NKVD also came for the writer Isaak Babel that same month.

Yet life went on for those still able to live relatively normally: Shostakovich sought teaching work at the Leningrad Conservatoire, and his old teacher Maximilian Steinberg obliged by finding him a position. Indeed, in early 1939 Shostakovich's professional life was, if anything, noticeably improved: in May he became Professor of Composition at the Conservatoire and he was also made a Deputy to Leningrad's City Council – a civic position carrying not very much power, but a significant amount of responsibility nonetheless. But the ongoing purges again came close to Shostakovich in June 1939. On his way back from a football match with Glikman, the two friends bumped into Meyerhold outside his flat and invited him in for tea. Now in dire straits and desperately fearful not only for his career but for his very survival, the theatre director was in far greater danger than he knew. The very next morning he was arrested,and never seen again by any of his friends. Shostakovich and Glikman were among the last people to see him alive, excepting his jailers and executioners. His wife, the actress Zinaida Raikh, wrote a petition pleading for his release, which Shostakovich is reputed to have signed. But to no avail; in July she herself was horrifically murdered in her own apartment. Meyerhold's disappearance and his wife's murder served as confirmation, if any were needed, that international fame was no protection. If Shostakovich ever hoped that, by being known in the West he might be safe from the ultimate fate, Meyerhold's arrest and Raikh's murder demonstrated that fame offered no sanctuary at all.

Though the symphony that Shostakovich was then composing, the Sixth, began with a bleak slow movement, the remaining two movements ranked among the cheeriest of Shostakovich's entire symphonic career. An opening *Largo* followed by two quick *scherzo* movements was already an unorthodox structure for a symphony, but the circumstances behind its composition make its high spirits even more enigmatic. When Shostakovich played the rumbustious finale to Sollertinsky and Glikman, Glikman went into immediate raptures over it, declaring that if Mozart or Rossini were alive they would have written something just like it; and Shostakovich himself offered the opinion that it was the most successful finale he had ever written. At the premiere in November 1939 the finale was encored and, even though critical opinion was divided over this strangely 'headless' symphony (the traditional first movement marked by its absence), and it was never officially regarded as a worthy successor to the Fifth, the Sixth Symphony escaped really serious criticism.

Yet how might we understand this paradoxical work – seemingly joyful, but composed in circumstances almost as horrific as those surrounding the Fifth Symphony? Certainly Shostakovich had no reason to feel completely secure: no one did. We know that during the worst months of 1937, as he was composing his Fifth Symphony, Shostakovich began spending nights waiting by the lift, so that when they came to arrest him, Nina and their baby would not be disturbed. He fully expected to be arrested; we know that he feared interrogation and torture, and considered execution a completely realistic possibility. He was in no way naive about the fate that awaited anyone who was taken in those years. We can only speculate on how he survived this horrific period of terror, and the effect on his mental state, but it seems possible that, once the most immediate fear had abated and his Fifth Symphony had been hailed as successful, Shostakovich found his way back to something approaching normality thanks to his family, friends, his new teaching work and through writing music. He had poured out a symphony of intense personal anguish and the way to healing – either for himself or for those around him – could not be found by repeating himself. Even if we hear the Sixth's finale as ironic or sarcastic, its explosive cheerfulness was assertive: it was a different response to pain and fear, but a no less powerful one than the Fifth had been.

Shostakovich's next work would have the happiest fate of all: it won him a medal, a large sum of money, enormous prestige and the means of concertizing with his new friends, the Beethoven Quartet. Composed in the summer of 1940, the Piano Quintet picked up on what was already a strong vein of classicism in Shostakovich's music and developed it to a high level of mastery. Although the rigorous Conservatoire training in seventeenth- and eighteenth-century compositional techniques like counterpoint, fugue and sonata form exasperated him as a student, Shostakovich was able to draw deeply on those skills when he needed to, and they were about to serve him exceptionally well. He had already used the baroque passacaglia form in *Lady Macbeth*; now his Piano Quintet would exploit baroque forms and textures even more prominently. Its opening Prelude immediately announces itself as distinctly neo-classical: then with the fugal slow movement and the slow stalking bass of the Intermezzo, Shostakovich made explicit what had been a key element in his style for a long time. The classical underpinnings of his technique, disparaged by him all those years ago to Yavorsky as impediments to his inner voice, now coalesced into a deeply personal language in which Shostakovich's classical training and his own voice at last found a perfect synthesis.

The timing of this synthesis was not entirely coincidental. One of the recurring criticisms levelled at Shostakovich in the wake of the 'Muddle Instead of Music' attacks was that he, like his fellow Soviet composers, needed to learn from the great masters of the past. The head of the Leningrad Composers' Union branch,

Shostakovich and the Glazunov Quartet performing the Piano Quintet, 1940.

Vladimir Iokhelson, called for Soviet composers to emulate the classics: Beethoven, Tchaikovsky, Musorgsky and Bach. Others demanded the purity and clarity of Mozart, Haydn and Gluck.[5] Though it may seem contrary to what we would expect from the stridently atheistic culture of Stalinist Russia, the 250th anniversary year of Bach and Handel (1935) had been celebrated warmly in Leningrad, with new performances of the Bach Passions and Handel's biblical oratorios. To emulate Bach was, in fact, a brilliant way of responding to *Pravda*'s criticism of *Lady Macbeth*'s 'formalism', because Bach was as 'formalist' an example from the musical past as could possibly be imagined, yet he was also untouchably great. To turn to the influence of Bach was infinitely preferable (politically speaking) to being influenced by Berg and Hindemith. Yet it was not a cynical shift: Shostakovich's embrace of Bach was timely, and probably considered in the light of all these factors, but it was to prove a critical lifeline over the next decade and indeed beyond, linking the Piano Quintet with the ultimate working-out of Bach's influence in the mighty first movement of the Tenth Symphony.

No sooner was the Quintet performed than it was nominated for the newly unveiled Stalin Prize. It seems incredible that this purely abstract piece of chamber music, not remotely glorifying to Stalin or even identifiable as Soviet, or Russian, would have won such a political accolade. What is more, Stalin had received a personal letter denouncing the Quintet from the critic Moisey Grinberg on 7 January 1941, who hoped to undermine Shostakovich's chances by going straight to the top:

> An atmosphere of unhealthy sensation has been created
> around the Piano Quintet by D. Shostakovich. Yet in its essence
> this is a composition of profoundly Western orientation
> (I mean the work of contemporary Western composers) . . .
> The first movement of the Quintet, it is true, is constructed
> in a classical, Bachian scheme. But how much there is
> in this quintet of stilted, singular new sounds . . . This is
> music that does not connect with the life of the people.[6]

Yet if Grinberg thought that Stalin, an opera aficionado, would care enough about his opinion of chamber music to take this letter seriously, he was wrong. As the musicologist Marina Frolova-Walker has shown, his letter went straight down the chain of command to the man who was then head of the Committee on Arts Affairs, Mikhail Khrapchenko.[7] It had no effect whatever other than to alert Khrapchenko to Grinberg's toxic behaviour – and to remain in Soviet archives for historians to discover decades later. Although it was not the case that the whole Stalin Prize Committee for Music unanimously praised the Quintet, Shostakovich did have very powerful supporters there, who very effectively swept away the reservations of musicians rooting for their personal favourites. The most outspoken was the artist Igor Grabar, who openly declared: 'When I was listening to Shostakovich's Quintet, I had the feeling that I was not among contemporary composers but among the great masters . . . This work is stamped with the seal of genius.'[8] Accordingly, in March 1941 Shostakovich won a First Class Stalin Prize for the Quintet, worth 100,000 roubles. A professor at the Conservatoire, a Deputy of Leningrad's City Council, a Stalin Prize winner and a father of two – Shostakovich was now every inch the establishment composer. At long last he might have begun to feel that the whirlwind had passed him by.

In late May 1941 Shostakovich let it be known that his next symphonic premiere would take place that year: his Seventh Symphony was announced in the Leningrad Philharmonic's 1941–2 season. That premiere did take place, but under circumstances that no one could then possibly have imagined, for on 22 June 1941 Hitler's armies invaded the Soviet Union, in a betrayal of the Nazi–Soviet pact signed in 1939. Despite being warned of the imminent invasion by Winston Churchill, Stalin, who mistrusted Britain far more than he did Adolf Hitler, had refused to take any preventative measures. Because of this, Hitler's troops advanced with alarming speed towards Leningrad, whose capture and destruction was a key Nazi war objective. Already partially encircled by later that summer, Leningrad was cut off from all evacuation and supply routes by September 1941 and was thus placed under siege conditions. By the time the blockade was lifted in January 1944 more than a million Leningrad citizens had starved to death.

Although Shostakovich had probably already begun mentally planning the Seventh Symphony before the invasion (or announcing its premiere in May would have seemed extraordinarily overconfident), he began written drafts only from July. By August he played the first movement to Glikman, commenting that the invasion theme itself – an innocent little piccolo tune that is at first ridiculous, but becomes ultimately terrifying – would probably spark unflattering comparisons with Ravel's *Bolero*. 'Well, let them,' Shostakovich allegedly concluded. 'That's how I hear war.'[9] By the end of August, elite political and cultural personnel were being evacuated, the Leningrad Philharmonia (with Ivan Sollertinsky) to Novosibirsk; Glikman departed too, to Tashkent. But Shostakovich refused to leave the blockaded city. He remained there until he was ordered to evacuate in September, by which time he had composed the second and third movements, the last a searing requiem for the dead and dying. Like the poet Anna Akhmatova, Shostakovich broadcast to his fellow citizens that September, telling them that he was still in the city, still composing.

On 1 October he was flown out with Nina and their two children to Moscow, and from there the family travelled by train to Kuibyshev (formerly, and now again, called Samara). But on arrival, conditions for the family of four were far too difficult to allow Shostakovich to complete the symphony. Squeezed into precarious and cramped living conditions with two excitable young children needing attention and care, Shostakovich also agonized continually about the fate of his mother and sister, Maria, who were still trapped in Leningrad. His anxiety was so intense that he wrote to Sollertinsky: 'Often at night, suffering from insomnia, I begin to weep. The tears flow abundantly and to hold them back is impossible for me. Nina and the children sleep in the other room so I don't disturb them. I often think of you and I can't do without your company.'[10] The artist Nikolay Sokolov, who socialized with the composer in Kuibyshev, reported that Shostakovich told him he had been unable to write the finale of the Seventh while the news from Leningrad and the front was so bleak. But then the tide turned: 'as soon as the news came through that the Fascists had been smashed outside Moscow, he sat down to compose in a burst of energy and excitement. He finished the Symphony in something less than two weeks.'[11] The finale of the Seventh was the most organically satisfying of all his symphonic finales to date. Building steadily towards its climactic ending, beginning from a serene starting point (the oscillating motif at fig. 189 that leads through to the coda), the finale sustains a slow but inexorable growth in momentum that is a masterpiece of symphonic pacing. The oscillating motif itself is drawn from an earlier theme in the finale, which is itself rooted in the symphony's grief-stricken slow movement (fig. 135), thus transforming mourning to victory in precisely the authentic manner Shostakovich had deliberately avoided in his Fifth Symphony finale. There, the victory was presented as hollow, but in the Seventh there is real hope. Yet though the positive ending captured the spirit of optimism that was so desperately needed during the war, Shostakovich confided in those close to him that the official reading of the Seventh Symphony had its limitations. To Flora Litvinova, their young neighbour in Kuibyshev, Shostakovich cautioned: 'music, real music, can never be literally tied to a theme. National Socialism is not the only form of Fascism; this music is about all forms of terror, slavery, the bondage of the spirit.' Litvinova told Elizabeth Wilson that later, when Shostakovich trusted her more, he informed her directly that the Seventh Symphony, and the Fifth as well, were 'about our system, or any form of totalitarian regime'.[12]

Unsurprisingly, Shostakovich kept these views within only his closest and more trusted circle of friends. The Seventh Symphony took on a life that was almost independent from its composer and became an icon of Soviet resistance to Hitler. Almost as soon as the work was finished and dedicated to the city of Leningrad it was flown on microfilm to the West, where the American conductors Leopold Stokowski, Serge Koussevitsky and Artur Rodzinski all tried to obtain first (Western) performance rights. In the end it was Henry Wood who gave the Western premiere at his London Promenade Concerts on 22 June 1942 – the anniversary date of Hitler's invasion of Soviet territory. But if the 'Leningrad' Symphony took on a propaganda role in the West, its significance to the city of Leningrad itself was incalculably greater. Though the prestigious Philharmonia had been evacuated, the Radio

Orchestra and its conductor, Karl Eliasberg, remained in the blockaded city. The orchestra itself had long since been disbanded, and very many of its players had been called up or had already perished from starvation. Calls went out for musicians to perform the 'Leningrad Symphony', with the promise of extra rations to help them regain the strength to play. Those who could be summoned from the front were brought back, and all those who could still play, however feebly, were set to rehearsal. Blockade survivors in the orchestra recalled that the weakened musicians never had the strength to play through the symphony in its entirety before the concert took place, and several of the players actually died after being recalled to perform. Yet on 9 August, Eliasberg and his Radio Orchestra performed the 'Leningrad' to an audience who could scarcely believe that, in the midst of so much suffering, they could really be sitting in the Great Hall of the Philharmonia on Nevsky Prospect listening to a symphony that had been dedicated to them.

Eliasberg's performance was relayed to loudspeakers positioned facing the Nazi encirclement positions and we know that the soldiers, as intended, found it both disconcerting and demoralizing. The conductor Semën Bïchkov reported that after the war, East German tourists who were returning to Leningrad after having been soldiers in Hitler's army sought out Eliasberg and told him that they had listened to the symphony as they surrounded the city:

> They went to see him and they told him they [had been] soldiers in the German army just on the edges of the city. They were listening to the broadcasts of that orchestra concert, including the seventh symphony of Shostakovich . . . They were hungry too. They were frightened as well. A lot of them didn't want to be there but had no choice. A lot of them got killed.[13]

They told Eliasberg that, on hearing Shostakovich's symphony, they understood the city of Leningrad would never be defeated. One former soldier actually told him that they wept as the music played.

Shostakovich's mother and sister finally arrived in Kuibyshev at the end of March 1942, so they were no longer in Leningrad to hear the historic performance. Reporting to both Sollertinsky and Glikman that his mother was wasted away to skin and bone, and evidently hugely relieved at having his family all together with him, Shostakovich nevertheless struggled to cope with the demands of wartime evacuation when Nina's extended family, including a brother-in-law whom Shostakovich did not much like, began to arrive at their apartment in Kuibyshev in the early summer of 1942. Confessing his anguish only to Sollertinsky, his most trusted friend, Shostakovich was painfully aware that complaints about evacuated in-laws did not sit well with his new image as the Soviet Union's most famous cultural icon:

I am living here with ten people. And there are more to come. The kind heart of my wife does not know any boundaries in gratifying these noble feelings. Soon her sister Irina Vasilievna will join us with her husband . . . and daughter . . . I don't blame Nina, because she, clearly, reasons differently when it concerns her relatives. She is a good person, but absolutely can't understand me on this issue. When I say to her, that if she thinks it possible to take in the troubles of such a colossal quantity of people, then would it not be better to bring from Leningrad for example Yevlakov or Boldïrev [both Shostakovich's composition students at the Conservatoire] since these people are having a very difficult time, with this she cannot agree, since Boldïrev belongs neither to my relatives nor to hers . . . Ivan Ivanovich, I have no friends here, with whom I can talk about this. So I am writing to you: I implore you, don't read this letter to anyone or reveal its contents. Now I have poured out my soul it feels easier, as Abr[am] Abr[amovich] Ashkenazy once said.[14]

But even as he struggled to cope with the loss of privacy and the strain of co-habiting with people he had no affinity with, Shostakovich suffered far more deeply from the absence of his friend Sollertinsky. Shortly before the deluge of guests, Shostakovich wrote to him, 'I miss you terribly – your company is as essential for me as the air I breathe',[15] and as he concluded his tale of *kommunalka* woes, Shostakovich confessed, 'Each day I dream that I will soon come to Novosibirsk and we will see each other after almost a year's separation.'[16] Though Shostakovich also wrote regularly to Glikman and clearly regarded him with immense affection, his letters to Sollertinsky in evacuation reveal a much deeper and stronger bond. When apart from his friend, Shostakovich's sufferings were profound. He was someone for whom different friends matched different parts of his personality, and each was treasured for the unique part they played in communing with his multifaceted character. And he was also someone who truly loved his friends: he placed an extremely high value on their loyalty, and would show equal loyalty in return. Sollertinsky was irreplaceable to him – an intellectual equal, funny, kind and loving – and in his letters to him Shostakovich shows a vulnerability that is almost entirely absent from any other written record of these years.

Unsurprisingly, Sollertinsky was one of those very few whom Shostakovich told about his next project. After completing the Seventh Symphony, he turned back to one of his favourite writers, Nikolay Gogol, and to his short humorous play about card sharps in a country inn, *The Gamblers*. Any more unlikely successor to the 'Leningrad' Symphony would be hard to imagine. Yet setting Gogol's deliciously wicked satire to music was balm for Shostakovich's soul – and perhaps an outlet, too, for his less than virtuous feelings towards his fellow men as he shared his home with Nina's brother-in-law. In the absence of his trusty librettist Alexander Preis, who had died in 1942, Shostakovich resolved that he would compose another opera based on Gogol, but this time set it word for word. This decision is probably what prevented him from ever finishing *The Gamblers*, because after composing 45 minutes of music, he was not even one-fifth of the way through Gogol's text. Yet he also realized that the composer of the 'Leningrad' Symphony could not possibly be seen to be working on such a frivolous project, even if, as was doubtful, the Soviet cultural climate would welcome such an opera. Gogol's play was, as his writing always is, darkly witty, but it was also piquantly appropriate for Soviet times, where the ugliest of human motivations could be paraded as grand civic sentiment. Such hypocrisy is beautifully illustrated in the exchange between the two characters Uteshitelny and Ikharev, as they discuss the noble art of cheating at cards: Uteshitelny asks: 'Should my own father sit down at the card table – I'd fleece him the same as I would any stranger. Who told him to play? At the card table all

Shostakovich and Sollertinsky during the war years.

men are equal'. To which Ikharev responds: 'Exactly! People don't understand that we gamblers may be the most virtuous of men.' Throughout Shostakovich's setting, thoroughly ignoble statements are set to hilariously expressive music, vividly recalling Major Kovalëv's searing rendition in *The Nose* of the line 'Last night I dreamed I had a pimple on my nose.' As Ikharev arrives at the inn and lovingly addresses his pack of cards, which he calls 'Adeleida Ivanovna', Shostakovich cheekily references Tchaikovsky's *Queen of Spades* in the drooping bassoon figure (in Tchaikovsky's opera, this accompanies the countess's dozing just before Hermann confronts her). And as Ikharev shaves, excitedly fantasizing about cheating the other guests ('I can't wait to do them over!'), his lyrical effusion is worthy of Tchaikovsky's Hermann himself.

Though rarely heard, and incomplete, the music Shostakovich wrote for *The Gamblers* shows that he had not lost a grain of his genius as either an opera composer or as a satirist. It also shows that he could happily slot right back into the worlds of *The Nose* and *Lady Macbeth*, regardless of the 'changes' in his musical style that the majority of his contemporaries had been shown since 1936. Shostakovich worked on his opera, orchestrating it and then making a piano score, until at least March 1943, writing only to Sollertinsky and Shebalin about it, and swearing them to secrecy. He knew this would never be anything other than his private project, fated never to see the light. Languishing bored in a sanatorium outside Moscow after falling ill with typhoid fever in January 1943, Shostakovich worked intensively on a number of smaller projects alongside his opera. Writing gloomily to Sollertinsky, he confessed,

> I am suffering from graphomania. I have written nearly all
> of a piano sonata, orchestrated my romances . . . made a
> piano score of my opera The Gamblers although it is far from
> finished and I will probably never finish it, but all the same I
> am continuing work on it . . . Apart from work . . . I feel bad

and don't know what to do with myself, although this is for a very small reason (that is, nerves and my bad character). I want to write you a cheerful letter, in order to cheer you up a little bit, but I can't. I'm not Irakly Andronikov [a charismatic Soviet media personality], nor respected artist of the republic Obraztsov [a puppeteer]. Don't be angry with me.[17]

The Second Piano Sonata, one of the fruits of Shostakovich's 'graphomania', does not wear its heart on its sleeve; even its slow movement refuses to indulge in any romantic pathos. All of the sonata, but especially the finale, again shows the influence of Bach at his most formal, with a somewhat dry, brittle and even severe character. It is written in the style of Shostakovich's own playing: unsentimental, unshowy and deceptively virtuosic. The 'Romances' Shostakovich refers to are the *Six Romances on Verses by W. Raleigh, R. Burns and W. Shakespeare*, each one dedicated to a close friend: Walter Raleigh's black-humoured poem 'To My Son' went to Levon Atovmyan, now released from the camps (since 1940); Robert Burns's 'O wert thou in the cauld blast' went to Nina and his 'MacPherson Before his Execution' to Glikman; Burns's whimsical 'Jennie' went to Shostakovich's student Georgy Sviridov and the folk song 'The Grand Old Duke of York' went to Shebalin. But the centrepiece was the setting of Shakespeare's Sonnet No. 66 'Tired with All These' in Boris Pasternak's translation, which he dedicated to Sollertinsky. Counting off those parts of life hardest to bear, the protagonist of the poem concludes:

And art made tongue-tied by authority,
And folly (doctor-like) controlling skill,
And simple truth miscall'd simplicity,
And captive good attending captain ill:
Tired with all these, from these would I be gone,
Save that, to die, I leave my love alone.

Whether Sollertinsky had introduced Shostakovich to these verses or not, the significance of these words was plain. Once again, an untouchable classic – now Shakespeare rather than Bach – provided Shostakovich with flawless cover. Such sentiments could never be written in a letter (everything was read, or at risk of being read, by censors), nor could they be openly voiced; but when they dated from a previous age, they were rendered safe. The sonnet's dedication marked the abiding closeness of their friendship, setting down in the musical record their complete and shared understanding of the times in which they lived.

That summer Shostakovich completed his Eighth Symphony, finishing it in September. Sollertinsky wrote soberly to his wife after hearing it in Novosibirsk: 'It is far more difficult and acerbic than the Seventh or Fifth Symphonies, and therefore it is unlikely to become popular.'[18] This would prove a stunning understatement. At the time Shostakovich composed the Eighth Symphony, the war had taken a decisive turn in the Allies' favour: Soviet forces had defeated Hitler's armies at the Battle of Stalingrad by January 1943 and Stalin, taking the title of Marshal of the Soviet Union and certain of victory, now assumed the rank of the Soviet Union's pre-eminent military leader. Officially, the rhetoric of war had shifted from solidarity in the face of shared suffering to assurance of victory. But Stalingrad had cost close to half a million Soviet lives; the city itself was utterly destroyed and fighting still continued. Though Shostakovich sought to protect his new work with anodyne statements, describing it as expressing his creative mood 'influenced by the joyful news connected with the victories of the Red Army',[19] colleagues were not so easily put off. In the same letter to his wife, Sollertinsky reported that the symphony immediately accrued a group of powerful enemies and in fact, after a hostile discussion about the work in the Composers' Union in March 1944, it was effectively barred from further performance. Despite Shostakovich's claim to have written an 'optimistic'

Shostakovich with Isaak Glikman, 1940s.

symphony, that was simply not what many listeners heard. Yet the Eighth does end in a gentle C major that could conceivably match the composer's description of its overall message: 'Everything that is dark and gloomy will rot away, and the beautiful will triumph.'[20] Shostakovich had voiced such a belief much earlier, in his setting of Pushkin's poem 'Rebirth' quoted in his Fifth Symphony: the image of the 'artist-barbarian' who disfigures a beautiful painting that, with time, is restored to its original purity as the 'alien paint' flakes off. The poem's closing words, echoed in the Fifth Symphony reference, ran: 'Thus do delusions fall away/ From my tormented soul/ And there spring up/ Visions of pure, clear, days.' Shostakovich's words about his Eighth were surely sincere, but what was 'beautiful' in his vision of hope? Evidently not the restoration of what had become normality under Stalin before the war. Writing to Glikman on New Year's Eve, 1943, Shostakovich observed caustically, '1944 is around the corner. A year of happiness, joy and victory ... The freedom-loving Peoples will at long last throw off the yoke of Hitlerism, and peace will reign throughout the world under the sunny rays of Stalin's Constitution.'[21] If the Eighth ended with a vision of grace lying beyond the present, it did so in defiance of Soviet expectations of pomp and bombast – and that defiance was only too audible to other musicians who were, perhaps, becoming attuned to Shostakovich's way of 'fulfilling' official expectations in perversely oblique ways.

Another critical milestone of Allied victory came with the lifting of the Leningrad blockade in January 1944. But just as the prospect of returning to their homes and work was raised, Shostakovich suffered one of the worst losses of his life thus far: Sollertinsky died on 11 February 1944 in Novosibirsk. The blow was incalculable: Shostakovich had no other friend to whom he could turn with personal troubles in quite the same trusting way, and he never formed another attachment as close as that to Sollertinsky. The last three years of their friendship had been marked by the pain of separation and now, after surviving Stalin's purges and war, they were denied the chance of returning to their old comradeship. Turning back to the Piano Trio that he had begun in December 1943, Shostakovich dedicated his new work to Sollertinsky's memory. Within just a few days of receiving the tragic news of his friend's death, Shostakovich had finished the first movement, but then abruptly stopped. By April, having got no further, he wrote to Glikman in despair at his writer's block; aside from writing the score for Arnshtam's wartime tragedy *Zoya* (based on the true story of a young partisan girl, Zoya Kosmodemyanskaya, who was captured and hanged by the Nazis), Shostakovich found that he was unable to work for months after his bereavement. Only when he had decamped to the new composers' retreat of Ivanovo for the summer did he manage to regain creative energy, finishing both the Trio and the Second String Quartet within two months. The Trio's second movement is, according to Sollertinsky's sister, a musical sketch of his character: robust, energetic, eccentric – full of positive energy and in places decidedly comical. After this most affectionate of tributes, the slow movement is a sombre leave-taking, expressing in music what even Shostakovich's own words could barely articulate: 'We shall not see him again. I have no words with which to express the pain that racks my entire being. May his memorial be our abiding love for him . . . Ivan Ivanovich is no more. It is very hard to bear.'[22] However, the Trio's finale seems to be about something quite different, and marks the start of a new element in Shostakovich's voice. Its dance-like character is unmistakeably Jewish in flavour, and not only that: its two main themes oscillate between a ghostly dance and a shrill, agonized response that eventually becomes the movement's furious climax. Though Shostakovich never explained the meaning behind it, the Soviet press was for a time filled with reports of Nazi atrocities in the death camps, including Vasily Grossman's report from Treblinka that guards had forced Jewish prisoners to dig their own graves and dance upon them. From this point on Jewish musical intonations would become an increasingly entrenched part of Shostakovich's musical personality, and in at least two subsequent works he would explore the theme of Jewish persecution explicitly.

Following the completion of his Eighth Symphony, Shostakovich was keenly aware of the symbolic significance that would be attached to his Ninth, following the symbolic importance of Beethoven's Ninth in the post-revolutionary era. What is more, the successor to this Seventh and Eighth Symphonies was supposed to be the final part of a 'war trilogy', and this time, a victorious offering could not be avoided. Indeed, expectations of a monumental Ninth were stoked by Shostakovich himself. As early as October 1943 he announced a 'large-scale work in which the overpowering feelings ruling us today would find expression. I think that the epigraph to all our work in the coming years will be the single word "'Victory.'"[23] One of Shostakovich's Soviet biographers, David Rabinovich, reported that the composer told him in 1944 that he had started work on the Ninth, which was intended to be written for orchestra, soloists and choir (following the model of Beethoven's Ninth), and Shostakovich also told his composition students in January 1945 that he had completed the first part. Glikman was treated to a piano performance of the first ten minutes of the new work, and described it as 'majestic in scale'.[24] Yet after an apparently promising start, Shostakovich found he could not go on with the Ninth as he had originally planned it. That summer he scrapped his drafts and quickly composed an entirely different symphony: short, lightly scored and as far from the 'majestic' apotheosis he had promised as could be imagined. Though the finished Ninth was far from a throwaway work, its first movement is perky rather than grandiose, and the all-important finale begins with a grotesquely humorous bassoon solo, giving the distinct impression of a fixed grin rather than genuine high spirits. As with the Sixth Symphony, popular reception was extremely positive, and the last three (out of five) movements were encored by audience demand at the premiere. Yet – also as with

First page of the pre-Ninth Symphony.

the Sixth – Shostakovich's colleagues were less enthused. A general
sense of disappointment at his failure to provide the expected
Soviet 'Ode to Joy' pervaded Composers' Union discussions, and in
time, as will be seen, punishment would follow.

Yet looking at the draft of the planned heroic Ninth, which has
now been published and recorded, it is clear that Shostakovich did
originally conceive of it as the natural successor to his previous two
symphonies. What we see is the outline of a symphonic conception
that eventually came to fruition in the first movement of the Tenth
Symphony. Though that work was not completed until 1953, and
is rightly considered a powerful statement of creative freedom in
the immediate post-Stalin era, there are clear motivic links with
the Ninth's draft score, and with another abandoned work from
this period: a sonata for violin and piano which has also been
published and recorded in recent years.[25] Shostakovich began work
on the sonata immediately after completing the finished Ninth
Symphony, and it too looks forward to the Tenth's first movement,
with a strong connection in particular to its third theme, which
(in the sonata) reveals its original Jewish inflections. In the sonata,
the theme is a Jewish-style dance with a gentle oom-pah piano
accompaniment below the violin's twisting dance-like melody.

These two abandoned projects tell us a lot about Shostakovich's
long-term thinking. Although the series of abandoned works
from the 1940s (including two more failed operatic projects, *The
Gamblers* plus plans with the Kirov for an opera on Tolstoy's novel
Resurrection, which was banned by the repertoire censor) suggest
that he was flitting from one idea to the next, in fact under the
surface a process of evolution was underway of which the composer
himself was probably not fully aware. Shostakovich had always
been intrigued by the challenges of symphonic pacing and he had
developed into a powerfully contrapuntal composer: his textures
are frequently more 'horizontal' than 'vertical', reflecting not
only his Conservatoire training and the influence of Bach (and for

that matter Hindemith during the 1920s and early '30s), but his admiration for Yavorsky's modal theories, which offered him a way of combining classical and modern techniques. When finally he was able to compose the first movement of the Tenth Symphony, widely considered the pinnacle of Shostakovich's symphonic achievement, its broadly paced canvas, deeply founded in Bach's polyphonic style, had been gestating for over a decade.

In the months leading up to Allied victory in September 1945 the Soviet Union had begun to position itself as a global superpower, laying claim to large parts of Eastern Europe in a massive expansion of the Soviet bloc and building up its own nuclear programme. Alongside geopolitical manoeuvres, however, Stalin initiated repressive domestic cultural measures, fronted by the Culture Minister Andrey Zhdanov. It was the literary world that found itself on the immediate receiving end of sweeping reforms: theatre and film soon followed. Musicians watched the unfolding tragedies with increasing alarm: when the distinguished poet Anna Akhmatova was publicly attacked and expelled from the Writers' Union it was clear that no one was to be deemed irreplaceable. Akhmatova was the Soviet Union's pre-eminent poet, despite suffering great personal loss under the Bolsheviks (her first husband Nikolay Gumilëv was shot by the Cheka in 1921 and their son, Lev Gumilëv, was arrested and sentenced to five years in the camps in 1938; he would be arrested a second time in 1949). Zhdanov also denounced the satirist Mikhail Zoshchenko as a 'vulgar philistine' obsessed with portraying the Soviet people in a negative light, and he too was expelled from the Union.[26] Deprived of any means of making a living from writing, Akhmatova and Zoshchenko were condemned to severe poverty and Flora Litvinova told Elizabeth Wilson that Shostakovich personally helped Zoshchenko with money at this time.

Against this grim background, Shostakovich continued, paradoxically, to thrive. Although some in the Composers' Union

had already begun to attack him – most memorably the critic Izrael
Nestiev who accused him of letting down the Soviet people with
the 'cynical, pernicious grotesquerie' of his Ninth Symphony –
Shostakovich was showered with honours and awards in 1946.[27] He
was elected Chairman of the Leningrad branch of the Composers'
Union (Vladimir Iokhelson's old job), given his third Stalin Prize
(for the Piano Trio), awarded the Order of Lenin in December
1946 and, in October 1947, as part of the thirtieth anniversary
celebrations, Shostakovich and his fellow composers Prokofiev,
Khachaturian, Shebalin and Yury Shaporin were named People's
Artists of the RSFSR (Federation of Soviet Republics). In time for the
revolutionary celebrations, Shostakovich dashed off an enjoyable
medley of popular tunes, his cantata *Poem of the Motherland*
– again falling well short of anything that could be described
as 'majestic'. Once again, as with both the Eighth and Ninth
Symphonies, Shostakovich's response to official demands was
apparently obliging but firmly on his own terms: the cantata neatly
circumvented any expectation of pomp by opting for lightweight
popularity. During the summer of its composition, Shostakovich
was concentrating on something much closer to his heart: the First
Violin Concerto, written for the Soviet virtuoso David Oistrakh.

One of Shostakovich's most popular works, the Concerto was
half-finished by the end of 1947, with two of its four movements
fully orchestrated: a brooding opening movement and a fleet-
footed scherzo in which a bold new note of self-assertion can be
found. The scherzo features a prominent four-note motif that first
spells out in notation the letters DSC (the first three letters of D.
Schostakowitsch in German spelling, with Es the German spelling
of E flat) with B flat at the end (so making DSCB). Near the end of the
movement this motif appears in various transpositions to give the
'correct' sharpened ending, which, at the right pitch, would then
spell DSCH (H = B natural in German notation). Though DSCH is not
found in the movement at its correct pitch, the motif's distinctive

shape, with the final semitone (C to B) rather than the original tone (C to B flat) is firmly established. The DSCH signature would recur with a vengeance in the Tenth Symphony, to a truly obsessive degree, but in the First Violin Concerto it is still embryonic: Shostakovich has discovered its potential and is playing with the idea but not yet fully realizing it.

By the time Shostakovich began work on the slow movement in the winter of 1948 (the concerto was completed by March) Andrey Zhdanov's attacks on the Soviet art world had turned to music. The concerto's composition thus spanned an extraordinary period of both honour and disgrace: begun by a composer decorated with multiple awards and prizes and completed after Shostakovich, once again, had been publicly disgraced and his works blacklisted. During the three-day meeting of composers in February 1948, Shostakovich was repeatedly denounced by fellow composers and his music ridiculed by Zhdanov as comparable to a 'musical gas-wagon'. He was forced to make two self-abasing statements to the conference – the first time he had ever been pressurized into doing so, as he had avoided any public address in 1936 – and the whole episode vividly recalled his previous humiliation and fear.

Old terrors that had receded, even if never forgotten, now resurfaced. Shostakovich once again kept a bag packed in readiness for his arrest. And though he was not arrested, we now know that his fear was not at all unfounded. As had been the case during the purges of the 1930s, international fame offered no protection; with the Cold War now well and truly established, the Soviet Union no longer needed to court Western opinion. Stalin's ghoulish NKVD head, Lavrenty Beria, had been Shostakovich's patron of sorts during and after the war: Shostakovich had written music for the NKVD Song and Dance Ensemble's wartime revues and Beria also interceded for Shostakovich with Stalin to obtain for the composer a new dacha, a large Moscow apartment and even a new car.[28] But even that did not guarantee survival. Beria's deputy, Viktor

Shostakovich with his children, Maxim and Galina, at the dacha in Komarovo, 1948–9.

Abakumov, had prepared Akhmatova's arrest warrant after forcing her son to admit (under torture) that she was hostile to the Soviet regime. Stalin never signed the warrant, but ordered Abakumov to continue surveillance.[29] Akhmatova's NKVD file was reportedly more than nine hundred pages long: a poet was in no way beneath Stalin's personal attention. There was no reason for a composer to be more fortunate. In 1970 Vano Muradeli, whose opera *The Great Friendship* served as the pretext for the whole *Zhdanovshchina* (the Zhdanov affair), granted an extended interview with the Moscow musicologist Vladimir Zak. According to Muradeli, Shostakovich in 1948, 'walked with the "noose around his neck". The executioners were standing by the gallows. According to my source, the file, revealing Shostakovich's "sabotage activities as an old Trotskyite and helper of Zionism" had already been prepared by the NKVD. They only waited for the "go-ahead".'[30]

Though Shostakovich's NKVD file, if it survives, has never to my knowledge been examined, and so Zak's account cannot be verified, this report is only too plausible. For it was made before Veniamin Basner revealed to Elizabeth Wilson that Shostakovich had been called for interrogation in 1937. It also takes account of Shostakovich's growing public sympathy with Jews, something that had become extremely dangerous in the viciously anti-Semitic years of late Stalinism. Zak quotes Muradeli as having told him,

> I know personally that he [Shostakovich] was under
> surveillance by the NKVD, as if he were a spy . . . When
> in January of '48 they killed Mikhoels, Shostakovich
> immediately came to his family, expressed his condolences,
> and spent a long time in this apartment. This was
> immediately 'noted', and reported where appropriate.[31]

We know that this reported fact was true: the great Jewish actor Solomon Mikhoels was murdered by the NKVD on Stalin's orders and Shostakovich knew his family well, since his friend, the composer Moisey Weinberg, was married to Mikhoels's daughter Natalia. Natalia told Elizabeth Wilson that Shostakovich came round to their apartment on the day of his murder and had said to her and Weinberg, quietly, so that no one else in the room could hear, 'I envy him' – neither he nor Mikhoels's family then understood that his death had not been an accident. This tallies, too, with Nina Shostakovich's distress, as reported by their friend Yury Levitin, when after Zhdanov's conference of musicians had ended, Shostakovich told her that he was considering suicide.[32]

Yet Shostakovich did not commit suicide. Remarkably, he found the strength to complete his violin concerto, telling Glikman that he worked steadily on the slow movement every evening when he returned from the conference. The movement itself was an extraordinary achievement, both musically and personally. Built on the passacaglia form that Shostakovich turned to for some of his most private and deeply felt utterances, it transforms the hurt and humiliation of those nightmarish days into one of the most dignified and beautiful slow movements he ever composed. Then, calling on all his reserves of positive energy as he had done with his Sixth Symphony, Shostakovich leads the passacaglia via a long and fiendishly difficult cadenza (in which the DSCH motif is again heard, as though struggling towards the light) into a brilliantly assertive finale. Although Shostakovich played the concerto to his students in March 1948, and David Oistrakh learned it the same year, neither composer nor soloist was sure that going ahead with the premiere would be wise and the concerto was put aside, not to be publicly performed until after Stalin's death.

As 1948 wore on Shostakovich's miseries increased: dismissal from his treasured posts at the Leningrad and Moscow Conservatoires came that September, and a list of his most 'formalist' compositions was blacklisted, with the result that nothing was played, even those works, like the Fifth and Seventh Symphonies, that were never banned. Royalty payments ceased and the Shostakovich family was plunged into poverty. Their loyal housekeeper Fenya and her niece spent their savings supporting them,[33] while Levon Atovmyan made suites from Shostakovich's forgotten jazz, theatre and film scores in order to bring in some much-needed income.[34] It was Shostakovich's turn to be helped, as he had helped others. Yet his now well-established survival strategy of appearing to do as required while suiting only himself remained unvanquished. He had one last trick up his sleeve for 1948: he spent the summer setting texts from a small volume of Jewish folk poetry that he had bought in 1947. Part of the resulting cycle, *Songs from Jewish Folk Poetry*, was performed at Shostakovich's home during his birthday celebrations in September 1948 by the husband and wife team of Sviatoslav Richter and Nina Dorliak. Subsequently, Shostakovich added three more songs to the cycle and, later that year, played them all to Nikolay Myaskovsky. An informal 'premiere' at Shostakovich's apartment took place in December, and Shostakovich's intention was to submit them for formal review at the Composers' Union Plenum that month. Yet it seems that he did not, in the end, do so. Even though the cycle was quite widely known, Shostakovich held back from a formal public premiere. His reasons for hesitating are not yet fully understood. On the one hand, the Jewish songs were an ideal example of the kind of 'folk' culture to which Soviet composers were being exhorted to pay homage. Other Jewish-themed works were passed and approved by the Composers' Union that year, including Weinberg's Sinfonietta, based on Jewish themes. But on the other hand, Shostakovich was not even slightly politically naive. He was also very alert to Soviet anti-Semitism, and perhaps he heard intimations of the coming crusade against 'rootless cosmopolitans' and 'Zionists' already by the end of 1948. This would seem plausible, since the anti-Jewish campaign was already in full swing in the Soviet press by January 1949, and from this time until Stalin's death on 5 March 1953 Soviet Jews were targeted in a new phase of political terror. Under surveillance, deprived of income, publicly humiliated, perhaps even with his arrest warrant drawn up by Abakumov, Shostakovich again came close to vanishing into the whirlwind.

4

Finding a Way Forward

If at the start of 1949 Shostakovich was in serious danger of arrest, the danger receded as swiftly as it had approached. On 16 March 1949 Shostakovich's friend Yury Levitin was visiting him and Nina. Shostakovich was feeling unwell, a state of affairs that had begun to be depressingly normal, and as Levitin sat with them, a call came for Shostakovich. It was Stalin. Nina and their other guest Anna Vilyams, wife of the painter Pëtr Vilyams, immediately hurried into the next room to listen on the second receiver, while Levitin listened to Shostakovich's replies. Stalin asked Shostakovich if he would join a delegation travelling to New York for the Cultural and Scientific Conference for World Peace, which would take place at the Waldorf Hotel in March that year. When asked about this phone call by his later biographer Sofia Khentova, Shostakovich reminisced:

> I imagined with horror how I would be pestered there with questions about the recent resolution and blurted out that I was sick, I couldn't go, and that the music of Prokofiev, Myaskovsky, Khachaturian and myself was not being performed. The next day, a brigade of doctors arrived and examined me, and really did pronounce me sick, but Poskrëbïshev [Stalin's secretary] said he would not relay that to Comrade Stalin.[1]

This whole episode, however, had been preceded by an official request that Shostakovich would take part in the delegation, to which the composer himself had responded very negatively. On 7 March 1949 Shostakovich wrote to Leonid Ilïchëv, the deputy head of the Central Committee of the Communist Party, enumerating his serious reservations about the trip (the letter is reproduced here in full for the first time):

They tell me that the American conductors S. Koussevitsky and A. Toscanini want to arrange concerts of my works to coincide with my visit to America. They want me to appear in these concerts as a soloist. As a soloist in symphonic concerts I can only appear with my piano concerto. However this concerto was written a long time ago and isn't the kind of work which can be played right now. I have many doubts about the idea of organizing such symphonic concerts. Koussevitsky has in his repertoire my Seventh, Eighth and Ninth Symphonies. Toscanini has the Seventh and, I think, the Fifth. Of these works, symphonies 8 and 9 are banned by Glavrepertkom [the repertoire censors]. So I don't see how symphonic concerts of my works can be organized, in which I myself am supposed to participate. If my appearance is really essential, then it would be better to organize a chamber concert of my works. I could perform my Quintet and Trio and a quartet could be played (one from the three). It would be highly desirable, if I am to perform in this concert, to play with the Beethoven Quartet. They have played all my chamber music often. In the event that my works would be played by some American ensemble, then it would be very difficult to devote enough time to [rehearsing]. Any public performance is a major strain on my nerves. I play rarely and do not have much stage practice. Apart from that, my health is consistently poor. I feel constant nausea. Doctors aren't able to advise me what it might be. I myself don't pay any attention to it. I assume it will pass. However, up to now it hasn't. Therefore a journey to America, to stay there, to play in concerts – all this would demand from me immense strength. I ask for your help in this matter. It would be easier if for this complicated and difficult journey my wife, Nina Vasilievna, could accompany me. She always comes with me on my travels and always alleviates all the burdens of the journey, preparations for the concerts and so on. Apart from this, if I am to play in concerts in America, it is essential that I have a tailcoat made.[2]

Ilïchëv sent this letter to Molotov, who passed it to Stalin on 16 March. That very day, Stalin did two things: first he phoned Shostakovich and spoke to him directly. Then he sent out a direct order, rescinding the repertoire censor's ban. But Shostakovich's attempt to salvage something positive from the trip – playing with the Beethovens and having Nina with him – failed utterly. Instead he was paraded alone before an audience of 19,000 people at Madison Square Gardens, where he played a piano arrangement of the scherzo from his Fifth Symphony. At the conference itself, Shostakovich was represented by an interpreter who read out a prepared speech denouncing the American 'warmongers' while the composer fidgeted compulsively in his seat. Precisely as he had feared, Shostakovich then faced hostile and insensitive questions about the recent condemnation of his music in Russia and made a statement about Stravinsky, a composer whose music he worshipped, that was pure Sovietese: '[Stravinsky] betrayed his native land and severed himself from his people by joining the camp of reactionary modern musicians.'[3] The spectacle of Shostakovich being forced to read out prepared speeches – for many, if not all, of those in the room listening were aware that the words were not his own – haunted some of the more sympathetic Americans present, including the playwright Arthur Miller and, though he was guilty of harassing Shostakovich with deliberately provocative questions, the Russian émigré Nicholas Nabokov.[4]

Shostakovich's humiliating appearance in New York marked the start of what would become a pronounced split between his official and private faces. He realized exactly what was expected of him in his role as Soviet delegate and he went through the motions dutifully, even though his discomfort was visible to more perceptive members of the audience. Over the next ten years Shostakovich had ample opportunity to polish his public persona, and he eventually perfected it to the point where it was absolutely convincing to anyone who did not know him fairly intimately. This apparent personality split, where Shostakovich seemed increasingly able to detach his real feelings from his public image, has sometimes been perceived in his music too. And there is no doubt that the immediate impact of the Zhdanov Decree can be felt in the series of more 'official' works he embarked upon. But it is not possible to draw a clear line between what works are 'real' Shostakovich and what are not. In the first place, Shostakovich assigned opus numbers to some works that we might find comparatively weak, and declined to do so for others that we might like more, making it impossible to find a gratifying alignment between our idea of what is 'good Shostakovich' and what the composer's may have been. Additionally, the works that Shostakovich went on to compose in the aftermath of the Zhdanov Decree are too diverse to be lumped together as somehow 'inauthentic' or 'official'.

Yet it is undeniable that he continued to write music that he knew could not be performed at the time. A fruitful way of seeing this apparent anomaly in his work might be to see him as following at least two, if not three, creative paths from 1948 until around 1960 which, though apparently divergent, in reality had points of overlap. Such overlaps can be seen in his more 'Soviet'-style music – upbeat, verging on the bombastic – that can be heard in not only his official cantatas and film scores, but the finales of his Violin Concerto and even the First Cello Concerto. Stylistic overlap with his cantatas and film music can also be heard in his operetta

Moscow, Cherëmushki of 1957, a work that, far from being 'Stalinist', emphatically belonged to the 'Thaw' of the early Khrushchëv years. The divergences are most starkly apparent in the darker music of those works he withheld, including the Lermontov and Pushkin settings of the early 1950s: the severe, introspective voice heard in those works was certainly absent from the Stalin Prize-winning blockbusters of the post-Zhdanov period.

On his return to Russia that spring Shostakovich embarked on two radically different projects: the Fourth Quartet, which remained unperformed until after Stalin's death, and the cantata *The Song of the Forests*. This was Shostakovich's first full capitulation to political pressure – the first work of his in which Stalin was directly referenced. According to legend, the cantata came into being after a chance meeting between Shostakovich and the 'approved' poet Yevgeny Dolmatovsky on a train journey. Taking the current political theme of reforestation as their starting point, Dolmatovsky and Shostakovich put together texts and music and, when the cantata received its triumphant premiere under Mravinsky in November 1949, it won him another Stalin Prize (first class) and plaudits from every quarter. The composer Galina Ustvolskaya, who went with Shostakovich to the premiere, recalled how the composer wept inconsolably when back in the sanctuary of his hotel room.[5] Yet for all his shame, Shostakovich had not written a bad work. When he heard it for the first time, Myaskovsky noted in his diary, '[it was] very simple, but fresh and vivid'.[6] And indeed, apart from the admittedly overblown final movement, there is some genuinely beautiful music in *The Song of the Forests*. Nor is it alien to Shostakovich's music in other works dating from that period. Apart from the strong links with his score for *The Fall of Berlin* (itself a true potboiler), the cantata references both Musorgsky and Rimsky-Korsakov at certain moments, and features what would become a new direction for Shostakovich's music: his evocation of nineteenth-century Russian music and of the old Russian folk-song style.[7]

Shostakovich's ability to salvage something of value from an experience he found painful was a valuable survival tactic. Since he had been forced to compose a Stalinist cantata, he would not waste the time and thought put into it. And so from this point on, for the next few years – extending even beyond Stalin's death – Shostakovich continued to explore these Russian folk elements in a series of vocal works, most of which are very rarely, if ever, heard today. He collaborated with the film-maker Grigori Kozintsev on the biopic *Belinsky* in 1950, writing a score rich in folk melody, and the following year Shostakovich composed two sets of Russian folk and popular songs for choir. The *Ten Russian Folksongs* were never graced with an opus number, but they are extremely fine settings nonetheless, among which the delicate and sorrowful 'The Cuckoo's Cry' and 'The Match' stand out as particularly lovely. The other cycle, *Ten Poems on Texts by Revolutionary Poets* op. 88, drew upon Shostakovich's lifelong knowledge of old revolutionary songs. As a child Shostakovich had heard crowds in the Petrograd streets singing them, and some he may well have heard sung at home. These were no sops to Stalin, but songs deeply rooted in the psyche of Shostakovich's generation; and for Russians who, like Shostakovich, came from families sympathetic to the idea of revolution, they had a profound and humane significance. And so, although the *Ten Poems* may superficially appear a cynical offering to Stalinist dues, they were emphatically not that: the oppression and suffering depicted in the songs was as poignantly relevant to Shostakovich's betrayed and abused contemporaries as it had been when the songs were addressed to the Tsar.

These two song settings demonstrate Shostakovich's life-saving ability to wrest good from bad, and in exploring this angle of Russian heritage, Shostakovich laid foundations for a shift in his style that, though ultimately short-lived and probably of limited use to him, saw him compose many works over the next few years in a markedly more 'approachable' vein, in which the Sixth Quartet

and the operetta *Moscow, Cherëmushki* also take their place. But
alongside this new direction, Shostakovich would also achieve
closure on the final working-out of Bach's influence on his musical
language that had begun in earnest with the Piano Quintet and
evolved slowly throughout the 1940s. In 1950 he served on the jury
for the First International Bach Competition in Leipzig, timed to
coincide with the two-hundred-year anniversary of Bach's death.
At this event Shostakovich made the acquaintance of the young
Soviet pianist Tatiana Nikolaeva, who took first prize at the
competition. Inspired by her playing, Shostakovich quickly began
work on a number of preludes and fugues that eventually evolved
into a full cycle of 24: Shostakovich's twentieth-century version of
Bach's 48 Preludes and Fugues. He showed them to Nikolaeva, along
with other works he was writing concurrently, and, she claims,
dedicated them to her, though not in writing.[8] When he finally
showcased them at the obligatory Composers' Union gathering in
May 1951, most responses ranged between lukewarm and actively
hostile. The distinguished pianist Maria Yudina, however, spoke up
bravely: 'Much of what is composed today has no life in it because
it lacks inner content, mastery and pathos. But we pianists are
eternally grateful to Dmitri Dmitrievich!'[9] The following year, when
Nikolaeva played a selection of them, largely to the same people
who had criticized them the previous year, they were well received
and from this point she and other Soviet pianists began to include
the Preludes and Fugues in their concert programmes.

At last, on 5 March 1953, Stalin died. As the Soviet Union
embarked on a period of ritualized mourning, Shostakovich's
mood was probably a combination of relief and anxiety, since at
first the question of succession was far from clear. In the months
and years just before Stalin's death, the fresh waves of arrests and
the new climate of anti-Semitism had terrorized Shostakovich's
circle of friends: Moisey Weinberg (Mikhoels's son-in-law) had
been arrested in February 1953 and Shostakovich wrote to Beria

interceding for his release, an incredibly courageous act. Nina advised Weinberg's wife to prepare a power of attorney document to enable the Shostakoviches to care for their seven-year-old daughter when, as seemed inevitable, her mother would be taken. In fact, one of the first things to happen immediately following Stalin's death was the release of not only Weinberg but many of those recently arrested. On 27 March the so-called 'Beria amnesty' ordered the release of all prisoners with a sentence of five years or less, women with young children, and men and women over 55 and fifty respectively.

Shostakovich's next major work, the Tenth Symphony, is generally, and rightly, understood as an expression of bold self-assertion because of the finale's triumphant repetition of his musical signature, DSCH (D, E flat, C, B natural, spelling D. Schostakowitsch). It seems likely that he began work on it in earnest only after Stalin's death, since dates given for completion on both the Tenth Symphony manuscript and in letters to friends place the work's composition to the summer and autumn of 1953 – Shostakovich's standard period for composing a major work. Yet Nikolaeva always maintained that Shostakovich played the first movement to her in 1951 – and asserted that she heard the other movements too before 1953. In the case of the second, third and fourth movements, Nikolaeva's memory was probably at fault, but she may well have heard Shostakovich play something resembling the first movement as early as 1951. As we have already seen, the abandoned sketches for the Ninth Symphony and violin sonata had clear motivic links with the finished Tenth Symphony first movement. And, given that the gestation of Shostakovich's symphonies could be extremely long (the Fourth being an obvious case in point), even if he set them down in writing quickly, the abandoned Ninth could well have begun to mutate into the Tenth Symphony as early as 1951. In any case, the Tenth Symphony received its premiere in December

1953 under Mravinsky. As with the Sixth and Ninth Symphonies, audience and press responses were warm, even if Shostakovich was subsequently forced to undergo what was by now a ritualistic trial of criticism and self-abnegation at the Composers' Union. The Tenth Symphony was, and is, perhaps his greatest symphonic work. There is no grieving slow movement, as there was in the previous four symphonies; instead, the symphony opens with a vast, broad canvas of contrapuntal symphonic writing building steadily to a devastating climax. Following a vicious scherzo and a dance-like third movement, Shostakovich returned to the challenge of a symphonic finale, this time with the experience of the First Violin Concerto under his belt. He had already conjured up the concerto's DSCH motif in the third movement, this time faithfully positioned at the correct pitch. Now in the finale, Shostakovich's musical signature took on gigantic proportions of self-assertion, echoing through every instrumental group, including, right at the end, over and over again on timpani tuned to DSCH. Though we might imagine that the message conveyed by this glorious overstatement was abundantly clear, it is perhaps as well that the Composers' Union discussions did not dwell on the motif's significance or its dominance, focusing instead on the symphony's alleged 'gloomy, introverted psychological outlook' and its lack of positive ideas.[10] Unlike Prokofiev, who tragically never got the chance to continue his career after Stalin (he died on the very same day as the dictator), Shostakovich could celebrate outliving the cruel dictator. Along with other Soviet citizens, he observed closely the events that quickly unfolded: the forming of a 'triumvirate' of Viacheslav Molotov, Georgy Malenkov and Beria; Beria's arrest and execution in December 1953 and Khrushchëv's rapid rise to the post of General Secretary, while Stalinist hardliners were demoted or pushed into retirement.

Another detail of the Tenth Symphony links with an aspect of Shostakovich's personal life that is still only partly known about, and that is his relationships with other women. We know that after their remarriage in 1935 Nina had sanctioned an open relationship and begun one of her own with Alikhanyan. Shostakovich did not have such a long-term second relationship, but he did maintain a frank interest in other women. The reason we will probably never know much about these dalliances is that, happily for Shostakovich (who felt very strongly about such disclosures), the women he fell in love with were discreet. In some cases there was no real 'relationship' to speak of; Shostakovich merely needed a temporary muse. So it was with the Tenth Symphony: while composing the second movement and mulling over the third, he initiated a correspondence with a former Conservatoire student, the 24-year-old pianist and composer Elmira Nazirova. Between April 1953 and September 1956 Shostakovich wrote her at least 34 letters, requesting her photograph and describing to her in detail the theme he intended to use in the symphony's third movement, which was constructed on her name. The theme, an arresting solo horn call (fig. 114) uses the pitches E-A-E-D-A, which spells out Elmira in the sol-fa system (letters of her name given in capitals): E-La-Mi-Re-lA. It was an especially felicitous theme, because it echoes the horn call in Mahler's *Das Lied von der Erde* (The Song of the Earth), Shostakovich's favourite Mahler work and the piece of music which he said he would choose to hear if he had only an hour left to live. Mahler's horn call had a rather sinister association: it represented the cry of a giant monkey from a nearby cemetery, which, as a traditional harbinger of death, causes fear among the townspeople. Writing to Nazirova in September 1953, Shostakovich explained the Mahler connection, thus confirming the 'Elmira' theme's dual purpose: it enshrined her, paying homage to what she meant to Shostakovich during these years, and at the same time symbolizing his own tragic fate. The 'Elmira' horn call sits alongside the DSCH motif, calming it as it reaches hysterical levels of compulsive repetition and bringing the third movement to a peaceful resolution. Shostakovich and Nazirova met rarely, since she lived in Baku, but he did apparently tell her that he dreamed of living with her quietly at his dacha and once, at the bottom of a letter, copied out a line from Lensky's Act One aria in *Eugene Onegin*, where he sings to his fiancée Olga 'I love you'. Yet when they met, his behaviour was awkward and shy – clearly, his preferred way of adoring Elmira was from afar. Their correspondence broke off in 1956 but they maintained a distant friendship for the rest of Shostakovich's life.[11]

In a cruel twist of fate, Shostakovich was very soon to find himself alone. Nina died in Yerevan, where she and Alikhanyan worked in their laboratory, in December 1954. Her death devastated the composer. The fact that their marriage had been an open one did not mean Shostakovich had not loved her dearly. In fact, he depended on her as his truest and most faithful friend, the person who had done most to shield and protect him from the day-to-day pressures that, as he grew older, he was less and less able to endure. Unable to bear living alone, Shostakovich quite quickly began trying to fill the chasm left by Nina's death. Despite his apparent confidence to Nazirova while Nina was alive that he dreamed of living with her, he does not seem to have actually proposed marriage to her. But it seems he was quick to propose to at least two other women at this time. The composer and former Shostakovich student Galina Ustvolskaya, who had long been the object of his affections, turned down his offer of marriage, though Shostakovich had gone so far as to ask his children how they would feel about it, suggesting he was relatively sure she would accept him.[12] Reportedly, he proposed to her twice. But Ustvolskaya was not the only recipient of a marriage proposal in the immediate wake of Nina's death. Another close female friend of these years, the composer Margarita Kuss, met with Shostakovich regularly and received loving letters from him, especially during 1953 – the very year when Shostakovich was apparently so wrapped up in his feelings for Elmira Nazirova. But his relationship with Kuss was completely different. She was no distant muse whose physical presence discombobulated him. They met regularly; Shostakovich visited her in her apartment and addressed her as 'darling' in at least one letter. They also appear to have spoken every few days on the phone wherever possible. After Nina's death Shostakovich proposed to Kuss several times, but she refused him, not because she did not love him but, as she explained herself, she was afraid of losing her own creative identity if she married him. In fact, she never married, and kept silent about their relationship until right at the end of her life, when she allowed herself a few reminiscences about the 'Mitenka' she remembered.[13] A further painful loss from this period was the death of Shostakovich's mother in November 1955 – another chapter of his early life closed.

Alongside these personal difficulties, the Soviet Union itself had entered a new phase under Khrushchëv, and Shostakovich would himself take part in the long, necessary but painful process of 'de-Stalinization' that began with Khrushchëv's speech denouncing Stalin's crimes at the Twentieth Congress of the Communist Party. After this speech, nothing would be the same again: Khrushchëv set on the official record the arbitrary and brutal nature of the Stalinist repressions, reading out pleading letters written from prison cells, and confirming the innocence of those tortured and killed. In 1955 Shostakovich wrote to the prosecutor-general about Meyerhold, asserting his innocence, his loyalty to the Soviet regime and his creative genius. Meyerhold was formally rehabilitated two months later. Yet though the immediate strain of living under Stalin had passed, and Shostakovich was able to see all the works composed during the years 1948–9 finally performed (the First Violin Concerto, *Songs from Jewish Folk Poetry* and the Fourth Quartet), he did not instantly embark on a new compositional phase of unfettered experimentation. Far from it: Shostakovich's musical style had always been fiercely personal and

Margarita Kuss.

individual. He never changed his music to suit anyone, with very rare exceptions (the Violin Concerto actually being one, where Oistrakh had asked Shostakovich to give him a breathing space before the finale). As a composer, Shostakovich had evolved under Stalinism in a particular way, and by 1953 that was simply who he was. That helps us to understand why he did not return to his more audacious language of the 1920s or '30s, and nor did he seek to copy innovations then in vogue in the West, such as Pierre Boulez's total serialism, or Karlheinz Stockhausen's electronic experiments (though he thought well enough of Boulez's *Le Marteau sans maître* to give a copy to Shebalin as a birthday present in 1959).[14]

Younger contemporaries would increasingly feel disappointed by Shostakovich's apparent devotion to his more 'accessible' style. Flora Litvinova took him to task for his sentimental *Five Romances on Verses by Ye. Dolmatovsky*, composed in 1955:

> 'Why did you write music to those texts?' I asked.
> Shostakovich replied, 'Yes, the songs are bad, very bad.
> They are simply extremely bad.' And I piped up again,
> 'But why did you write them?' He answered, 'One day
> I will write my autobiography, and there I will explain
> everything, and why I had to compose all this.'[15]

But to Litvinova and others of her generation there was no convincing reason why Shostakovich 'had to' write anything. Times had changed, nothing would happen to him: he was free, surely, to compose exactly as he wished? However, it was not so simple. Until around 1958 Shostakovich was still on the path he had embarked upon in 1948 and he could not quickly change direction. He had said to the composer Andrey Balanchivadze in 1936 that 'If you find out sometime that I have "disassociated" myself from *Lady Macbeth*, then know that I did it 100 per cent honestly. But I think that this won't happen very soon . . . I am slow-witted and very honest in my work.'[16] The same is true in the post-Stalin period. Shostakovich had committed himself to a particular mode of composition for much of the period 1948–58. With the exception of the Tenth Symphony, Preludes and Fugues and his Lermontov and Pushkin settings (1950, 1952), he stuck to the more accessible style he had embarked upon after *The Song of the Forests*.

This adherence to a more 'official' style went hand in hand with another episode in Shostakovich's life that puzzled and upset many of his friends. Unable to persuade any of the women he truly loved to marry him, in the summer of 1956 Shostakovich fell almost by accident into a second marriage with a woman – Margarita Kainova – whom he had only just met and who worked for the Communist youth organization, the Komsomol. According to a friend during those years, Lev Lebedinsky, Shostakovich regretted his proposal the moment she accepted it. Though Lebedinsky was not always the most reliable of memoirists, his story of Shostakovich's muddled proposal is only too believable: called to Shostakovich's apartment to meet Margarita, Lebedinsky reported that, on her departure, Shostakovich confessed he had just proposed to her. 'Why on earth did you do that?' he enquired. 'Well, that's what has happened and I can't get out of it now' was Shostakovich's reply. Pressed on whether he was in love with her, Shostakovich mumbled 'no'.[17] Their marriage took place just a few days later. Everyone was baffled by Kainova's appearance in Shostakovich's life: they seemed to have literally nothing in common, and did not really even know each other. They were not friends; she apparently disliked his children and she understood nothing about his music. A less qualified substitute for Nina could hardly be imagined. Their marriage struggled on for three years and then, in a bizarre situation that echoed Tchaikovsky's abandonment of his own wife Antonina (leaving his brothers to remove her from his home), Shostakovich's sister Maria performed the same service for her brother, aided and abetted by Maxim. Their divorce went through apparently without incident, and nothing more has ever been revealed about the whole affair.

Margarita Kainova, Shostakovich's second wife.

Several key works date from the years of Shostakovich's marriage to Kainova. One is his Eleventh Symphony, which commemorated the 1905 massacre of peaceful civilians outside the Tsar's Winter Palace in St Petersburg. Shostakovich composed it in 1957, around the same time as he agreed to write the operetta *Moscow, Cherëmushki*. For his portrayal of that fateful day, 9 January 1905 (Old Style Julian calendar), Shostakovich returned to the revolutionary songs of his childhood, and not for the first time: he used 'You Fell as Victims' for the funeral of the fictionalized Kirov in *The Great Citizen* (1939). He also drew upon his recent choral work *Ten Songs on Texts by Revolutionary Poets*, specifically for the quoted song 'Bare Your Heads' ('Bare your heads/ On this sorrowful day'). Different generations responded differently to the symphony. Alexander Solzhenitsyn was scornful of Shostakovich's quoting from the old Tsarist-era song 'Listen!' ('Like a treacherous deed, the act of a tyrant/ the autumn night is black/ But blacker than night, there looms up from the mist/ the dark vision of the prison'). Zoya Tomashevskaya told Elizabeth Wilson how, at the premiere, many audience members were critical of the new work, saying 'He has sold himself down the river. Nothing but quotations and revolutionary songs.' But Anna Akhmatova, who attended the premiere with Tomashevskaya, responded deeply to hearing them: 'Those songs were like white birds flying against a terrible black sky.'[18] Her generation understood what the songs represented: for them, their association was not tarnished by their appropriation under Stalin. They remembered what the revolution – that of the Provisional Government in February 1917, even if not the Bolshevik Revolution in October – stood for, and what it had achieved. For those, like Akhmatova and Shostakovich, who grew up in those years, the songs had both a powerful nostalgic and ethical force. When one repressive regime replaces another, the people are still repressed: and that, over and over again, was Shostakovich's message in these works of the 1950s that revisit revolutionary themes.

Another meaning later attached itself to the Eleventh Symphony, which was that it was not about 1905 at all, but rather the Soviets' brutal crushing of the Hungarian Uprising in 1956. Tomashevskaya heard at second hand from the choreographer Igor Belsky that Shostakovich had inferred to him that the Hungarian Uprising was in his mind when he composed the symphony. Lebedinsky gave a more direct testimony: 'What we heard in this music was not the police firing on the crowd in front of the Winter Palace in 1905, but the Soviet tanks roaring in the streets of Budapest.'[19] Yet this seems not only disrespectful to the memory of those who fell under fire from the Tsar's troops all those years ago, but an opportunistic attempt to salvage Shostakovich's reputation as a moral voice at a time when it was being questioned. The frozen stillness of the symphony's opening in its 'Palace Square' movement is too evocative, and the soft entry of 'Listen!' on two flutes too powerfully linked with 1905 for this moment to be about anything other than the dawning of the fateful day in St Petersburg when so many lost their lives. This is not to say that the Eleventh could not have a double meaning: it certainly could, and very probably did. But we must also be open to the thought that Shostakovich deliberately, though not dishonestly, began the rumour that the Eleventh was about the Hungarian Uprising, and that he did so because he was aware that his symphony had disappointed people, especially the younger generation. It is entirely plausible that he composed the work with the two events paralleled in his mind and that he revealed the 'second' meaning in private conversation when he realized that his intentions – to cast light on the present from the lessons of the past – had not been guessed.

The second major work that Shostakovich wrote during his ill-fated marriage was one that he himself never really much liked: the operetta *Moscow, Cherëmushki*, which premiered on stage in January 1958. Given the multiple abortive opera projects of Shostakovich's career so far, from *Orango* and *Narodnaya Volya* in the 1930s to his beloved wartime project *The Gamblers*, there is a rather sad irony in the fact that the only operatic work Shostakovich would complete after *Lady Macbeth* was an operetta that he felt ashamed of. Yet it was a classic work of the Khrushchëv era: a gentle satire on Moscow's housing crisis, which Khrushchëv would attempt to solve with a hurried building programme of low-quality high-rises that came to be known disparagingly, though often affectionately, as 'Khrushchëvkas'. As rehearsals began, Shostakovich wrote to Glikman in December 1958:

> I am behaving very properly and attending rehearsals of my operetta. I am burning with shame. If you have any thoughts of coming to the first night, I advise you to think again. It is not worth spending time to feast your eyes and ears on my disgrace. Boring, unimaginative, stupid. This is, in confidence, all I have to tell you.[20]

Cherëmushki's release in a film version in 1962, however, makes the show as the composer saw it available to us, and reveals the brilliance of much of Shostakovich's score. The film itself is dated, as we would expect; but in certain respects it was rather daringly contemporary, with a brilliant dance sequence featuring the two main characters, Boris and Lidochka, dressed in late 1950s beatnik style, jiving on the beam of a crane as Shostakovich quotes from the well-known popular song 'Moscow Nights' (renamed 'Midnight in Moscow' when taken up by Kenny Ball and his Jazzmen in 1961).

However, it was during the later 1950s that Shostakovich began to feel the first intimations that there was something seriously wrong with his health. In September 1958 he wrote to Glikman,

> I have to stay in hospital until the beginning of October . . . My right hand is really weak. I have pins and needles all the time. I can't pick up anything heavy with it . . . When I write, the hand gets very tired. I can only play slowly and pianissimo.[21]

This was a serious blow to someone who was not only a phenomenal pianist and who relied on his pianism for demonstrating new works, but a right-handed composer used to doing all his own orchestration and piano reductions. From this point on, Shostakovich would find himself in and out of hospital, having a range of ailments treated.

He would eventually be diagnosed (though not until 1969) as suffering from a form of poliomyelitis, a condition that was difficult, probably impossible, to cure, though later Maxim was informed that Shostakovich actually had motor neurone disease.[22] By now used to poor health, no doubt in large part dating back to the nervous strain of the purge years and exacerbated by the war, Shostakovich was dismayed to find himself with the beginnings of serious disabilities. He had always found hospital stays boring; now they would become a regular feature of his life. During one such prolonged stay, in February 1960, Shostakovich completed his Seventh String Quartet, begun the previous summer, which he dedicated to Nina's memory. Like the Sixth Quartet, it begins with a jolly first movement, but the second movement immediately turns in an introverted direction, its shrouded second theme sounding stifled and cold. Following a violent fugato, the quartet concludes with a winsome, graceful waltz. If the Second Piano Trio had captured Sollertinsky's character in its explosive second movement, then perhaps Shostakovich meant something of Nina's youthful girlishness to be heard here.

If for much of the 1950s Shostakovich was working through the effects of 1948, with this quartet and his other major work of this decade, the First Cello Concerto, he finally broke free from its influence. Shostakovich wrote it for Mstislav Rostropovich, who, with his wife Galina Vishnevskaya, had become a trusted friend. Right from the start genial and playful, the concerto is nevertheless a far cry from most of the music Shostakovich wrote in the 1950s, and in many ways a much tougher piece than the First Violin Concerto. In that work Shostakovich had to work through ongoing painful circumstances and the optimistic finale was fiercely hard won. In the Cello Concerto Shostakovich's voice is grittier, less introspective perhaps, and certainly less tragic in its slow movement, but it is fired by a new type of creative energy. In every respect, the occasion of the concerto's composition and premiere was positive: released from his awkward second marriage and

Shostakovich with Rostropovich and Richter.

having finished what he knew was one of his most successful major works for a long time, Shostakovich had found in Rostropovich not only a good friend but a supremely talented musician and interpreter of his music. The 1950s had started exceptionally badly and had brought with them much sadness and loss: despite encroaching health problems, the decade ended on a new note of hope and confidence.

5

The Inner Gaze

If Shostakovich spent much of the 1950s working through the effects of the Zhdanov Decree and coming to terms with his adoption of a more establishment persona, the 1960s would present even greater challenges. He was already the recipient of multiple international honours by the end of the 1950s: invited to be an honorary member of the Accademia Nazionale di Santa Cecilia in Rome, awarded Commandeur de l'Ordre des Arts et des Lettres in Paris, given an honorary doctorate at Oxford University and given the Sibelius Prize in Helsinki. At home Shostakovich continued to climb the establishment ladder: he was made People's Artist of the USSR in 1954 and, even more prestigiously, awarded the Order of Lenin in 1956. Trips abroad to the West, the privilege only of highly favoured and trusted Soviet citizens, became frequent and high-profile: a return to the United States in 1959 for a tour of major cities and performances of his music showed that Shostakovich was regarded as a cultural figure who brought considerable prestige to the Soviet Union. He was also increasingly powerful within the Composers' Union, elected to its Secretariat in 1956 and made First Secretary of the Composers' Union of the RSFSR (as distinct from USSR, which Tikhon Khrennikov headed) in 1960, apparently at the express wish of Khrushchëv. In addition to being decorated with awards, Shostakovich was by now comparatively wealthy and both he and his family were entitled to privileges granted only to the Soviet elite. The comparison with his impoverished plight in 1948 could hardly have been any greater.

Shostakovich and Khrushchëv.

It hardly needs to be said that such official privileges came only with substantial strings attached. While Shostakovich shored up his professional status to the benefit of himself and his family, which quickly grew to include grandchildren, he simultaneously weakened both his former status as moral spokesperson for his contemporaries and the degree of personal integrity that came with it. That this was a trade-off with obvious implications would have been clear to Shostakovich: official power and status within the Soviet regime meant that one's 'unofficial' standing among the intelligentsia fell. Precisely how Shostakovich dealt with this and came to terms with it, if he ever did, is something we can never really know. Like many major cultural figures who had lived through the purges of the 1930s, Shostakovich's actions were shaped at least in part by fear. Oistrakh once confessed to Vishnevskaya that, in the apartment block where he lived, every single tenant barring himself and his wife and the people living in the flat opposite theirs were arrested during 1937. Having kept a bag packed in the event of his own arrest, which seemed inevitable, Oistrakh vividly remembered the night when a Black Maria pulled out outside the building and they listened to the lift coming upstairs, stopping on their floor: 'Whose door would they come to? An eternity passed. Then we heard them ring at the apartment across from us. Since that moment I have known that I am no fighter.'[1]

It is hardly surprising that Oistrakh, along with a great many other prominent musicians and cultural figures of their generation, applied to join the Communist Party. Shostakovich had managed to avoid Party membership but by 1960 his non-Party status was beginning to jar with his official image. Though it has never been

Shostakovich in 1958.

proven, Glikman's claim that the order to inveigle Shostakovich into joining the Party had come from Khrushchëv seems plausible. In any event, Shostakovich's eventual consent came at great personal cost. Both Glikman and Lebedinsky – and indeed both of Shostakovich's children – confirm that Shostakovich was devastated by his capitulation to pressure to join the Communist Party. Maxim Shostakovich remembered that when he called them in to tell them about it, it was only the second time in his life he had seen his father weeping (the first being after Nina's death). Lebedinsky suspected that Shostakovich was tricked into signing the application for membership by an official seeking to further their own career; Glikman even named the official as Pëtr Pospelov, who was indeed an ambitious functionary of the Communist Party, a candidate for election to the Presidium of the Communist Party and, as a former devotee of Stalin, no doubt anxious to strengthen his position in the new administration. Glikman reports that Pospelov gradually wore Shostakovich down with arguments and entreaties, trying to persuade him that it was his duty to support Khrushchëv's new regime and in particular to do all he could for music in which, Pospelov claimed, Khrushchëv was especially interested. Shostakovich confessed to Glikman that he eventually gave in to Pospelov but subsequently decided to resist by refusing to attend the meeting in Moscow at which he would be sworn in. On the eve of the meeting Shostakovich fled to his sister's flat in Leningrad and hid there. Lebedinsky claims that he prevented Shostakovich from taking the night train to Moscow and made him send in a telegram pleading illness. This proved an entirely fruitless attempt to avoid the inevitable: though that meeting was cancelled because of Shostakovich's absence, another was quickly re-scheduled. Glikman reports that Shostakovich turned up at his mother's dacha late at night three days later, clutching a bottle of vodka, and began talking about his fate, quoting Pushkin, 'There's no escaping from one's destiny'. Sure enough, Glikman says, Shostakovich attended the re-scheduled meeting and read out his prepared statement. Lebedinsky was harsh in his depiction of Shostakovich as a loyal Soviet public servant: 'Without fail he attended every possible ridiculous meeting of the Supreme Soviet, every plenary session, every political gathering, and even took part in the agitprop car rally. In other words, he eagerly took part in events which he himself described as "torture by boredom".'[2] Glikman's analysis was more perceptive: 'The utter fearlessness Shostakovich had exhibited in his creative and artistic life coexisted with the fear Stalin's terror had bred in him.'[3] Although Glikman and Lebedinsky, who had himself been a Party member since 1919, understood Shostakovich's revulsion at the prospect of Party membership, a great many of their friends had long since joined without comparable feelings of distaste and had even assumed that Shostakovich was himself a long-standing member. For some, joining was merely a pragmatic step, but for Shostakovich it felt like a moral death.

Shostakovich's musical response to this fresh trauma was immediate. In just two weeks he wrote his Eighth String Quartet and dedicated it to his own memory. In a letter to Glikman, he wrote,

> I wrote this ideologically flawed quartet which is of no use to anybody . . . The title page could carry the dedication: 'To the memory of the composer of this quartet' . . . I tried a couple of times to play it through, but always ended up in tears.[4]

Lebedinsky claimed that Shostakovich intended to commit suicide after writing the quartet by taking an overdose of sleeping pills: though his story is contested by other sources, it would not have been the first time that the composer seriously considered ending his life. The quartet quotes extensively from Shostakovich's past works (First, Eighth and Tenth Symphonies, Second Piano Trio,

Cello Concerto and *Lady Macbeth*), Siegfried's funeral music from
Wagner's *Götterdämmerung* and Tchaikovsky's Sixth Symphony,
plus the old revolutionary song 'Tormented by Grievous Bondage'.
Additionally, the work is founded on the DSCH motif, making
Shostakovich's self-identification with this work as explicit as
possible. After a doleful opening movement, DSCH is put to violent
use for a scherzo as rage-filled as that of the Tenth Symphony; the
climactic quotation of the Jewish dance theme from the Piano Trio
seems to suggest Shostakovich's inner fury at being made to dance,
like the victims of Treblinka, on the grave of his own self-worth.
With the fourth movement's quotation of 'Tormented by Grievous
Bondage' Shostakovich again, as in the Eleventh Symphony, draws
a comparison with the oppression of Tsarist times. In the quotation
following it, Shostakovich recalled Katerina's loving words to
Sergey in *Lady Macbeth* just as she is about to be cruelly betrayed:
'Serëzha, my darling, I've gone the whole day without seeing you'.
Shostakovich found listening to the work almost too painful to bear.
When the Borodin Quartet played the work for Shostakovich at his
home in 1960, he left the room at the end without speaking. The
next day he phoned the cellist Valentin Berlinsky and apologized:
'I'm sorry, but I just couldn't face anybody. I have no corrections to
make, just play it the way you did.'[5]

The link with *Lady Macbeth* was peculiarly timely. For although
Shostakovich had already made substantial revisions to his opera
– enlisting Glikman's help in reworking the libretto as early as
March 1955, none of the plans to perform it since Stalin's death
had come to anything. When he first submitted the revised score
for review in 1956, the Composers' Union rejected it harshly; then
the Kirov (formerly Mariinsky) Theatre planned it for their 1958
season and never followed through. But after Shostakovich joined
the Communist Party things began to change. It was not until
June 1961 that he got the official backing from the Composers'
Union that he needed to take the revival forward, and, under its

old Moscow title of *Katerina Izmailova*, *Lady Macbeth* was finally re-staged in a revised version in 1963. When Shostakovich quoted from it in 1960, very few people – perhaps only Glikman, whose memory of the opera had been refreshed by his recent collaboration with Shostakovich – would have recognized the lines he heard in the fourth movement. We can only guess at the meaning behind the self-quotation: was Shostakovich thinking of a lost love, a rejection, a betrayal or a lost chance of personal happiness? Katerina was already a lost soul by the time she sang those lines, about to be utterly betrayed and on the brink of her own suicide. If Shostakovich truly was planning to end his life after writing the quartet, then perhaps this was his identification with his heroine: when there is really nothing at all left to live for, then death seems the only choice.

Since Shostakovich did not commit suicide after joining the Party, he had only one other option: to fulfil his obligations as a Party member. And it feels like an act of supreme cognitive dissonance that, on finishing his Eighth Quartet, he embarked on the most 'official' of all his symphonies. Lebedinsky's account of the Twelfth Symphony's composition is exaggerated, but makes a colourful story: according to him, Shostakovich planned the Twelfth as a satire on Lenin and composed it from beginning to end. Then, at the last moment, he realized that it could not possibly be performed, and so he scribbled out another in about three days. Lebedinsky then went with him to the rehearsal, and related events as follows: 'The music was frightening in its helplessness. I experienced some terrible moments, and I thought I was about to go mad. Shostakovich was holding my hand, and he kept asking "Is it really awful?"'[6] In another account, Lebedinsky dated the composition of the 'new' Twelfth to two weeks before the premiere on 1 October 1961 – better than three days, but still implausible.[7]

From letters to Glikman, we know that Shostakovich was writing the symphony in the summer of 1961, though he had already broadcast programmatic details of the new work on the radio in October 1960, claiming that two of its movements were almost ready.[8] Though it may indeed be the case that he began the symphony again from scratch in the summer of 1961 and wrote it very quickly, the final Twelfth was not a rushed job by Shostakovich's normal standards. Given that Weinberg and Boris Tchaikovsky gave a four-hand piano performance at the Composers' Union on 8 September and a detailed description of the work, based on study of the full score, was published on 16 September, the symphony could not have been finished a few weeks before the premiere. Indeed, we know that Shostakovich finished the Twelfth on 22 August and had prepared the piano version by 25 August, ready to give his friends plenty of time for the run-through. Altogether it seems most likely that Shostakovich sketched the Twelfth in 1960 but re-wrote it substantially in the summer of 1961. Further – to spoil Lebedinsky's story even more – the Twelfth is far from the hack-work that he implies. Thematically, it is very carefully planned and from beginning to end it sounds every bit like a symphonic work by Shostakovich, echoing the Eleventh in particular in several places. The ending, following the admittedly bombastic 'Dawn of Humanity' theme (yet consider the equally bombastic finale of the Seventh, or even of the Tenth), is a very powerful echo of the Fifth Symphony's final pages, with the same leaning upon the minor sixth degree, the same dominant–tonic timpani, and the same idea of a repeated gesture stringing out the coda to unnatural length. Shostakovich had used these kind of endings before too, in *The Great Citizen* score of 1937: they were in his compositional DNA.

But how do we explain Lebedinsky's determination to distance Shostakovich from the Twelfth Symphony by both claiming that the original (abandoned) work was a satire on Lenin rather than a tribute, and that the official, finished symphony was a rushed job by a composer who realized too late that his satire could not be performed? As it happens, the gist of Lebedinsky's story, though demonstrably false in crucial details, does have one unexpected endorsement, and we find it in the private diary of Isaak Glikman. Attending a rehearsal of the Twelfth, Glikman – who felt lukewarm about the symphony barring only the first movement – could not avoid showing his lack of enthusiasm to Shostakovich when asked for his opinion: 'D. D. was very upset by my comments . . . Shifting in his seat, he suddenly blurted out: "I will tell you a secret. I wrote this symphony in ten days." This probably wasn't true, but he evidently felt a need to justify himself.'[9] It is not inconceivable that Shostakovich made some ironic comment to Lebedinsky about the symphony being a 'satire'; nor is it inconceivable that Shostakovich, when abandoning his drafts (assuming he did not merely re-plan the work and use a lot of the original material, which is also possible), rejected a more radical plan and wrote a more conventional symphony very quickly. Though Lebedinsky's exaggeration over the last-minute rewrite can be dismissed, the essence of his story – Shostakovich's rejection of his original conception and rapid composition of a less satisfactory work – cannot be brushed aside, and Shostakovich's own, no doubt also exaggerated, comments to Glikman give the tale further credence. Once again perhaps he sensed that this new work would disappoint some valued friends and, as he had done with the Eleventh, attempted to head off serious criticism by creating distance between his 'real' self and the apparent ideological conformity of the work's programme. If Shostakovich had spun a similar line to Lebedinsky, this would explain the origins of his tall tale.

Many of Shostakovich's contemporaries were disappointed with the new symphony. Part of the reason some heard it as quite so compromised was that it was unveiled almost in precise tandem with the long-awaited premiere of his Fourth Symphony in December 1961, the parts of which had languished in the Leningrad Philharmonia library since they were put away in 1936. Levon

Atovmyan found them there in 1961 and reconstructed the score; Shostakovich, on reading it through, announced that he would not change a single note. He had never entirely given up hope of having it performed: he had made a two-piano score of it and might have been able to reconstruct the full score had he wished to (though there is no evidence that he ever considered doing so). In a letter to Glikman from hospital in September 1958, he had confessed: 'I think about *Lady Macbeth* and the Fourth Symphony. I should so like to hear both of these works performed . . . I don't have very high hopes of either work being performed, but I indulge myself by hearing them in my inner ear.'[10] In 1961 Shostakovich was so affected by hearing his long-lost symphony that he told both Lebedinsky and Glikman that he considered it his finest work; or at least better than his most recent symphonies (in which he included the Eighth, which he had until then regarded as his best). Flora Litvinova, who attended the premiere, wrote in her diary afterwards, 'Why do Dmitri Dmitrievich's later works lack those qualities of impetuosity, dynamic drive, contrasts of rhythm and colour, tenderness and spikiness?'[11] It was a sad reflection from a friend; but perhaps, looking back on Shostakovich's career as a whole, we might now disagree with Litvinova's assessment. She had been frustrated by the apparent taming of the composer she got to know during the war, whose every musical utterance seemed to her a sacred act. She would have had in mind the Dolmatovsky Romances that she had disliked; been aware, at least, of *Moscow, Cherëmushki*; and perhaps also included the Eleventh Symphony in her mental list of disappointing Shostakovich opuses. The truth was that he had simply gone in a different direction; Litvinova may not have known the Cello Concerto, which is most certainly as spiky and dynamic as anything Shostakovich had composed in the 1940s, but it is true that his voice had altered.

The fact was that Shostakovich had begun, inexorably, to turn inwards. The Cello Concerto's slow movement shows the beginning of this enigmatic, even remote, tone in his music; the Seventh Quartet's slow movement shows it too. The counterweight to that turn was a different kind of extroversion in his symphonic music, of which the Twelfth is an especially strong example. But that outward-facing quality, which we might think of as 'civic' in orientation rather than personal, is a feature also of the Eleventh Symphony, and it would recur in his next symphony, the Thirteenth, as part of a major statement on civic responsibility and ethical principle. Therefore it is not the case that we should read these later works as introverted = authentic, extroverted = inauthentic, however tempting it might be to do so. We can only guess at how these different sides of Shostakovich's musical personality might be reflected in him as a person: certainly, he had been brought up in a family whose concern for others was selfless. His parents sheltered those in danger of political persecution, regardless of their ideology, and involved themselves in petitioning for those who had been arrested both pre- and post-1917. After Shostakovich had experienced political persecution himself, he came to place an incalculably high value on loyalty, integrity and care for others. During the purges Shostakovich wrote music that reflected the terror of those years; during the war he reflected the agony of human loss and the desperate hopes for peaceful resolution. Now, in Khrushchëv's 'Thaw', he did something different again: he reflected his era's groping after sincere and humane values, whether they were to be found in revolutionary ideals or whether, as in the Thirteenth Symphony, they were to be found in challenging existing problems in Soviet society. We might even conceive of the Eleventh to Thirteenth symphonies as a kind of 'civic' trilogy, typifying the soul-searching of Soviet society during de-Stalinization and, at least with the first two works, embodying the call of those years 'Away from Stalin, back to Lenin.'

Before he embarked on the Thirteenth Symphony, however, Shostakovich's personal life took a decided turn for the better.

Since 1960 he had known Irina Supinskaya, a young literary editor at the Soviet musical publishing house who worked with him on the vocal score of *Moscow, Cherëmushki*. They became friends and started seeing each other regularly. In June 1962 they began living together, and they married that November. At long last Shostakovich had found a true friend to live by his side and, in time, help him cope with the many challenges that old age threw at him. It seems paradoxical, perhaps, that this new happiness did not obviously translate itself into his music which, if anything, continued to grow more austere over the last thirteen years of his life. But the 'inner' Shostakovich and his official persona remained – had to remain – utterly apart from each other in these years. He was never First Secretary of the Composer's Union (of the USSR) – that position had been held by Tikhon Khrennikov since 1948 and he did not relinquish it until well after the fall of the Soviet Union. But aside from Khrennikov, Shostakovich was probably the most powerful and influential Soviet composer of his time, a status bestowed on him by his Party membership, and for which he paid constant dues in the form of attending meetings, reading speeches that seemed not only genuine but often truly enthusiastic, and signing all manner of official requests and documents, usually without even reading them (sometimes his signature appeared upside down, signifying his total lack of engagement). A contented marriage gave him a peaceful home life, but it could not bring these split halves of his life together, and his way of coping was, at least in part, to keep the 'public' side of his musical language ethically based.

When the young Soviet poet Yevgeny Yevtushenko published his poem 'Babi Yar' in the journal *Literaturnaya gazeta* in September 1961, he faced an immediate wave of anger. He had recently travelled to the site of a Nazi atrocity near Kiev, where more than 100,000 people – mainly Jews – had been murdered and thrown into a ravine (Babi Yar was the name of the ravine). To his distress, Yevtushenko found no memorial at the site: all attempts to have one

Shostakovich, Kondrashin and Yevtushenko after the premiere of the Thirteenth Symphony.

erected were thrown out under Khrushchëv's leadership. Therefore his poem addresses this directly, opening with the words 'There is no memorial at Babi Yar'. It goes on to commemorate persecuted Jews in twentieth-century history, from Alfred Dreyfus to Anne Frank, taking in pre-revolutionary pogroms and ending with the lines, 'I am every old man shot dead here/ I am every child shot here/ No part of me can ever forget this./ Let the 'Internationale' ring out/ When every last anti-Semite on earth/ is buried forever.' Just as these words were anathema to Khrushchëv's anti-Semitic policies and the powerful vein of anti-Semitism that ran through Soviet society, they struck an immediate chord with Shostakovich. By the time he phoned Yevtushenko to ask his permission to set his poem to music, he had, in fact, already done so: he had begun it almost as soon as he had read the published poem.

Having initially planned Babi Yar as a stand-alone movement, Shostakovich quickly found that he wanted to extend it into a full-scale symphonic work. He chose four more Yevtushenko poems

– 'Humour', 'In the Store', 'Fears' and 'A Career'. In a letter to his student and friend Boris Tishchenko, Shostakovich explained why the poetry, which Tishchenko found preachy and irritating, was so important to him:

> To remind us of it [ethical principles] over and over again is the sacred obligation of man . . . Every morning, instead of morning prayers, I reread – well, recite from memory – two poems by Yevtushenko, 'Boots' and 'A Career'. 'Boots' is conscience. 'A Career' is morality . . . To lose conscience is to lose everything.[12]

This confession is revealing. Shostakovich had found his representative of contemporary Soviet morality in Yevtushenko. Though sacked for doing so, the *Literaturnaya gazeta* editor Valery Kosolapov had sanctioned the poetry's publication and Shostakovich seized the opportunity to add his voice to Yevtushenko's and to use his official heft to give added weight and influence to what the young poet was trying to achieve. It was a rare

Shostakovich and Kondrashin discussing the Thirteenth Symphony.

pairing of generations: the 57-year-old composer and the thirty-year-old poet joining forces in one of the boldest public statements of the Khrushchëv era.

Unsurprisingly, the symphony did not have an easy premiere – in fact, it was almost not performed at all. Following Khrushchëv's angry reaction to the 'Manezh' exhibition in December 1962, and his summoning of artists to a meeting in the Kremlin to discuss the future of Soviet art, the composer Dmitry Kabalevsky advised Shostakovich to cancel the premiere of his new symphony. And indeed, the very next day Shostakovich was summoned to a Central Committee meeting where pressure was applied directly to cancel it.[13] Shostakovich's first choice of bass, Boris Gmyria, turned down his invitation, frankly explaining that his own position was not secure enough to withstand the likely political fallout. Mravinsky would also turn Shostakovich down, with Kirill Kondrashin taking his place. With Viktor Nechipailo secured as Gmyria's replacement and Vitaly Gromadsky as his stand-in, rehearsals began in December 1962. Right on the eve of the symphony's premiere, Yevtushenko and Khrushchëv actually had a face-to-face argument over anti-Semitism at a meeting of politicians and cultural figures. Then Nechipailo failed to appear for the dress rehearsal. When Gromadsky took his place, signalling that the performance was going ahead after all, Shostakovich and Kondrashin were asked to withdraw the symphony; Kondrashin reported a phone conversation where he was asked if the first movement could be omitted. Despite all these pressures, the premiere went ahead and was crowned by a passionate ovation.

Notwithstanding Yevtushenko's later capitulation to pressure to alter the strongest and most accusatory lines of his poem, the success of the Thirteenth Symphony seems to have re-energized Shostakovich. In the years immediately preceding his third marriage, the composer had been at an exceptionally low ebb. In a letter to Glikman from November 1961 Shostakovich alludes cryptically to 'this particularly difficult moment of my life, which has already dragged out its existence far too long'. In the same letter, he revealed that he had completed his Ninth Quartet, but destroyed it: 'I finished the Ninth Quartet, but was very dissatisfied with it so in an excess of healthy self-criticism I burnt it in the stove.'[14] What remained of this work was only found in 2003: a single movement in more or less finished condition. Hearing it now – and particularly if we compare it to the Ninth Quartet that Shostakovich completed in the summer of 1964 – we might feel that he had been right to discard it. The surviving movement has a strikingly grim, unlovable tone: stentorian, severe and emotionally boxed-in. But the Shostakovich of 1964, despite his failing health, was a much happier man than he had been in 1961. He dedicated the finished Ninth Quartet to his young bride; if the Eighth, privately dedicated to himself, had brought the composer to tears of despair, then the Ninth feels reawakened to life. It is a work full of positive energy, not tragic, confiding, nor even especially intimate in tone, but infused with both sweetness and a sense of Shostakovich's sheer pleasure in his own powerful technique. The finale is a stylistic tour de force, with aggressive fugal writing, 'oriental' dance-like passages and a cadenza for solo cello that prefigures similar passages in the later Second Cello Concerto, using pizzicato chords to interrupt the solo line. In a typically enigmatic comment to a *Pravda* reporter, Shostakovich alleged that the quartet was 'a children's piece, about toys and going out to play'.[15] While this seems a classic piece of meaningless evasion, in fact there is an intriguing link with childhood in the quartet's third movement, which, at its centre, quotes a sweet, childlike melody that we hear in the film score for Kozintsev's *Hamlet* (1963–4) as Hamlet, holding Yorick's skull, reminisces about how he used to play with the king's old jester. And the plaintive quality of the Ninth Quartet's opening has a similar childlike limpidity that would become a recurring feature of Shostakovich's late style. That quality is there most strikingly in the beautiful flute duet opening of the Thirteenth Symphony's finale, 'A Career', as well as in that movement's ending. If Shostakovich was brushing off the *Pravda* reporter with a facile comment, there was perhaps more than a grain of truth in it; but increasingly in his later music it feels inappropriate to expect any work to be 'about' anything in particular. As we will come to see, Shostakovich's 'late style' differs sharply from his middle period precisely in this quality of evasion.

So then, together with the Tenth Quartet, which he wrote later that same summer, the Ninth Quartet marks a sharp turn away from the confessional tone of its predecessors. The fundamental good-naturedness of both works is not a mask: it is balanced out by exploration of quartet timbres that were totally new for Shostakovich. The Tenth's second movement, for instance, delivers an astonishing display of deliberate ugliness: crude, heavy repetition of the simplest rhythmic figures, with dissonant double-stopped chords grinding against them. Then, in the spirit of Beethoven's beautiful *Canzona* from his next to last quartet, No. 15, op. 132 (Hymn of thanksgiving from a convalescent to the Deity, in the Lydian mode), Shostakovich turns straight to his favourite passacaglia form, with a lamenting, archaic flavour, full of open fourths, before concluding with a playful Allegretto. Never before had Shostakovich's stylistic range been so wide in any quartet. There is nothing predictable here, just as there is nothing emotionally readable. Having pushed the confessional quartet to its limits in the Eighth, Shostakovich used the Ninth and Tenth to re-assert his mastery of the genre.

If these 'abstract' works allowed him to give full rein to his formidable technique, though, Shostakovich had not turned away from the civic themes that had dominated his last three symphonies. Having completed these quartets, he put the finishing touches to his third – and by far his best – cantata, *The Execution of Stepan Razin*. Although Western audiences tend not to know this work, as it is rarely performed, it forms part of a long and very distinguished history of Russian culture celebrating the seventeenth-century Cossack hero. Composers and artists of the stature of Glazunov (*Stenka Razin*, 1885), Vasily Surikov ('Stepan Razin Sailing in the Caspian Sea', 1906) and Kustodiev ('Stenka Razin on the Volga', 1918) were attracted to the Razin legend. The famous Russian bass Fëdor Chaliapin frequently performed the popular nineteenth-century song about Razin, underlining the extent to which his story took on greater dimensions of folk heroism in late nineteenth and early twentieth-century Russian culture. Though guilty of savage violence, Razin became a Russian folk hero because he mobilized ordinary Russians against the Tsar's forces, playing on popular grievance against the boyars and the recent imposition of serfdom. He was betrayed by treacherous fellow Cossacks, tortured and executed horribly in front of a crowd: the few surviving eyewitness accounts testify to his courage and refusal to indict fellow rebels.[16] Shostakovich, still deeply interested in Yevtushenko's poetry, chose his recently published verses about Razin for the cantata's text, though freely cut lines he regarded as weak or unsuitable. Though he hated the real-life brutality of his cantata's subject, and several times questioned Razin's suitability as the subject of another 'civic' work because of it, in the end the appeal of Yevtushenko's setting proved irresistible. The poem is a classic 'present in the past' Soviet allegory, showing the fallen hero – betrayed, arrested and tortured – spat upon by the jeering crowds, who are apparently incapable of understanding that he, not the Tsar, is their true champion. In the seconds before his execution, both Yevtushenko and Shostakovich freeze-frame the scene: as the reflections of boats in the Moscow River glint upon the axe, and Razin looks at the faces of those in the crowd, we hear the same ominous, but beautiful, stillness of the Eleventh Symphony's opening pages: this time not Palace Square as the Sun rises on 9 January 1905, but a suddenly stilled crowd on Red Square, about to witness another atrocity. The spirit of revolution hangs over Razin at that moment: by linking his murder to those of the 'Bloody Sunday' massacre of 1905, Shostakovich honours him as the first link in a revolutionary chain of resistance to power.

Stepan Razin is also Shostakovich's most explicit evocation of Musorgsky in any work. Given that he had undertaken a full re-orchestration of *Boris Godunov* in 1940, of *Khovanshchina* in 1958–9 and of his *Songs and Dances of Death* as recently as 1962, he was deeply immersed in Musorgsky's musical and ethical worlds. Musorgsky's influence is especially clear in *Razin*'s orchestration (low strings outlining a heavy melody below swirling violins), in the chiming of the Kremlin bells, but also in the final message itself. As Razin's severed head mocks the Tsar, both Yevtushenko and Shostakovich claim allegiance to the same ethical message: power is ultimately weak, because it is corrupt. The only power worth having, though it may cause your own death, is moral power. Just as Pushkin ends *Boris Godunov* with the triumphant announcement of the Pretender's accession to the throne, with the treacherous boyar Mosalsky crying 'Long live Dmitry Ivanovich!' followed by the famous concluding indictment 'The people are silent', Shostakovich and Yevtushenko likewise show that, after Razin's murder, a silence falls over the crowd. The Tsar is victorious, but he has lost his people's respect and loyalty. Writing to Glikman, Shostakovich observed, 'I have written the poem in *style russe*. Critics both favourably disposed and hostile will find plenty of material to occupy them . . . Not to mention that the whole idea of the piece is essentially depraved.'[17] *Stepan Razin* was, indeed, yet another of Shostakovich's double-edged civic statements: on the one hand both quintessentially 'Russian' and Soviet in his celebration of this revolutionary folk hero; on the other standing in solidarity with all those who find themselves on the wrong side of power.

As Shostakovich was completing *Stepan Razin*, another seismic shift in Soviet politics took place: Khrushchëv was ousted in

October 1964 and replaced by Leonid Brezhnev. What this meant for Soviet culture as well as for ordinary Soviet citizens did not become clear until February 1966, when two writers, Andrey Sinyavsky and Yuly Daniel, were put on trial for agitation and propaganda against the Soviet Union and sentenced to seven and five years respectively in hard-labour camps. This apparent return to the show trials of the 1930s was a profound shock, especially for a younger generation who had never experienced the Stalinist terror and had come of age under Khrushchëv's much milder regime. Such was the determination to resist this new hard-line culture that the trial kick-started other forms of subversive activity (Sinyavsky and Daniel had been publishing under pseudonyms abroad): *samizdat* (self-publishing; manuscripts circulated and copied between friends) and *tamizdat* (privately circulated manuscripts from the West). In music there was even a *magnitizdat* (banned forms of music circulated and copied on tape or old X-rays). Though Shostakovich sympathized with the younger generation, urging his friends to read Alexander Solzhenitsyn's landmark publication *One Day in the Life of Ivan Denisovich* in the heavyweight journal *Novy Mir* in November 1962, and supporting Yevtushenko, he participated in what we now call the 'dissident' movement of the 1960s only in the most tangential way. His great civic statement – the Thirteenth Symphony – was his one and only brush with the post-Stalin administrations. Galina Vishnevskaya recalled that he repeatedly tried to dissuade both her and Rostropovich from getting too involved in political affairs: 'Don't waste your efforts. Work, play. You're living here, in this country, and you must see everything as it really is. Don't create illusions. There's no other life. There can't be any. Just be thankful that you're still allowed to breathe!'[18] In 1956 Shostakovich had suggested to friends that his Eleventh Symphony was as much about the Soviet crushing of the Hungarian Uprising as about 1905. But under Brezhnev he made no further attempts to align himself with intellectual protests against the government. Any sympathy or solidarity he expressed in his later music with younger dissidents such as Alexander Solzhenitsyn would be so oblique as to be almost invisible.

This apparent failure to engage as a critical Soviet citizen frustrated younger contemporaries who had grown up seeing him as a moral authority figure. Time and again Shostakovich presented a stolidly official face as he performed his duties; he could not even be relied upon to oppose the First Secretary of the Soviet Composers' Union Tikhon Khrennikov, for example, when younger composers – even those he supported and liked – faced his petty jealousy and determination to suppress their careers. Shostakovich's advice to Vishnevskaya and Rostropovich suggests that he chose to focus his remaining strength, for his health was rapidly failing him now, on maintaining loving relationships with family and close friends, working with the musicians he valued and continuing to create music so long as he was able to. Occasionally he had the satisfaction of being able to help someone in need – to speak up for a younger composer, to help someone financially in need, to support a constituent needing somewhere to live – but as he grew older and weaker he began to pare down his activities to what, for him, were the fundamentals: composing, working with musicians, and trying to absorb as much positive energy as he could from his increasingly restricted life. Always fond of travelling, he and Irina took extended holidays to places of great natural beauty, including Lake Baikal and the huge primal forest between Belarus and Poland, the Białowieża Forest (Belavezhskaya in Russia). In his later letters to Glikman, Shostakovich wrote of his burgeoning fascination with the natural world: 'Lately I have begun to share some of Yevgeny Mravinsky's traits, like a love of nature,'[19] and noting:

Of late I have become passionate about nature, I expect because so much of it has now become inaccessible to me.

My poor shattered legs do not work very well, and I can walk only with difficulty. Forbidden (and inaccessible) fruits are the sweetest. So now I am ecstatic about all the little streams, glades, breezes, flowers and berries.[20]

These fragments of insight into his personal life are essential for understanding Shostakovich's late music. He had always been creatively resilient, but he had a protective personal characteristic too: a robust sense of humour and an ability to focus on beauty and positivity when surrounded by ugliness. In his music, beauty took many different forms: during the Stalin years we hear it most distinctively in his elegiac and tragic music (the ending of the Fourth Symphony; the slow movement of the Fifth and the Pushkin Romances (especially 'Rebirth'); the love music from Act Two of *Lady Macbeth*) and, in the Khrushchëv era, in his most gentle music, such as the *Ten Russian Folk Songs* (especially 'The Match' and 'The Cuckoo's Cry'). Some will hear it in the slow movement of his Second Piano Concerto, which has a heart-on-the-sleeve lyricism. But from around 1962 onwards, a new tone emerges with a quality of purity that was only rarely glimpsed earlier. The 'childlike' simplicity of the Thirteenth Symphony's finale (the opening and ending in particular) is one such moment; perhaps the closest relative to that kind of limpidity can be heard only in the ending of the 1936 Pushkin setting 'Rebirth', with its gentle rocking octaves. For Shostakovich, this poem of Yevtushenko's ('A Career') was a kind of ethical credo: at least for a short time, he made a habit of reciting it to himself on a daily basis. Just as the poem provided him with a moral anchor point, he was able to compose music for it that expressed hope: that looked itself squarely in the face and believed in its own integrity.

To some extent this quality of purity overlaps with the 'childlike' themes explored in the Ninth Quartet, at least in its genial opening and the quotation from *Hamlet*. But there the resemblance ends; for another important emerging feature of Shostakovich's late music, which we also hear in the Ninth Quartet, is that of simplicity exaggerated to truly grotesque proportions. This is taken to even greater extremes in the Eleventh Quartet: its second movement opens with a theme so simple as to be ridiculous, and it is immediately 'made strange' (after the Russian Formalist idea, popularized in the 1920s, of *ostranenie*, which later became more familiar to Western audiences as Bertolt Brecht's *Verfremdungseffekt*) by the string glissandi rounding off each phrase, a sinister echo of the cartoon-image drunken folk singer, who rounds off his lines with 'Ekh!' The finale recalls this theme in a chastened variant that is no less grotesque for its apparent innocence. But by far exceeding anything else written in this 'simple-grotesque' vein is the second movement of the Second Cello Concerto, based on the vulgar Odessan street song 'Bubliki', which Shostakovich seemed to have as an earworm since the New Year of 1966, where he unexpectedly picked the song as his favourite tune in a game with Vishnevskaya and Rostropovich. He began the concerto in February and completed it in April.

Both of Shostakovich's Cello Concerti have elements in common, which is hardly surprising given that they were both written for Rostropovich's powerful, charismatic personality. Yet the Second immediately steps away from the genial world of the First, with a lyrical, though subdued, opening movement more similar to that of the First Violin Concerto or even perhaps in places Berg's Violin Concerto of 1935. Right at the end of the movement another influence can be heard, one especially dear to Shostakovich's heart. Benjamin Britten had travelled to Russia and visited Shostakovich several times in Moscow since the two composers met in London in 1960: in 1963, on Britten's British Council visit; in 1964 to hear Rostropovich perform his own Cello Symphony; in 1965 and again in 1966 over New Year. Unable to converse freely owing to the language barrier, both men nonetheless drew close to each other through their music and through deep mutual professional admiration. And right at the end of the Concerto's first movement, Shostakovich evokes a sound world intimately associated with Britten: the high-pitched horn over sustained strings instantly brings the 'Elegy' from Britten's *Serenade for Tenor, Horn and Strings* to mind (a setting of William Blake's 'Oh rose, thou art sick' from *Songs of Innocence and Experience*).

Stepping with demonic relish into the realms of the extreme grotesque, the Second Cello Concerto's second movement subjects 'Bubliki' to fantastical exaggeration and distortion, complete with eccentric string glissandi and deliberately unidiomatic writing for bass woodwind (bassoon and contrabassoon), forcing them to cluck dementedly at the top of their range as 'Bubliki' is pressed through yet another distorting variant. But it is actually in the finale that Shostakovich truly surpasses himself as a master of the grotesque: after the climactic return of 'Bubliki', punctuated with whip-strokes, the music seems to become music about ending as much as about its own strangeness. In rapid succession we are presented with a delicate neoclassical cadence, complete with trill, an evocation of the inner workings of a machine (whirring and ticking effects produced by tom-toms, side drum and woodblock) and the cello's eccentric harping on a falling minor third glissando. Not since *The Nose* had Shostakovich composed anything quite so disorientating. And whereas in his opera the grotesquerie makes total sense in the realization of Gogol's story, in the concerto we have literally nothing to grasp; no way of easily making sense of what any of these half-comical, half-sinister gestures might mean.

Among the more dubious pleasures of Shostakovich's old age was the frequency with which he found himself besieged by official awards and honours. Though on one level recognition always pleased him, he felt ambivalent about his awards too, disliking the ceremonies that he had to endure and, no doubt, also feeling some embarrassment about their inevitability for such a pillar of the Soviet musical establishment as himself. He received two prestigious awards on his sixtieth birthday: Hero of Socialist Labour and the gold medal 'Hammer and Sickle'. Almost as though anticipating them, Shostakovich had already provided an ironic counter-award four months earlier in the shape of his self-deprecating squib, *Preface to the Complete Edition of my Works and a Brief Reflection Upon this Preface*, for which he wrote the text himself. With no pretensions to poetic glory, Shostakovich drily concluded with a self-mocking list of his various honorific titles: 'Dmitry Shostakovich/ People's Artist of the USSR/ Followed by many other honourable titles/ First Secretary, Composers' Union of the RSFSR/ Plain old Secretary of the Composers' Union of the USSR/ As well as very, very many other quite important responsibilities and positions.'

Though the self-mockery is frequently recognized, it is certain that Shostakovich also intended the targets of his *Preface* to extend well beyond himself. At the words 'This is a Foreword that might be written/ not only for my Complete Works/ but also to the complete works of very, very many other composers', the melody leans wittily on 'very, very', just in case any hearing the *Preface* failed to see that they too were the butt of Shostakovich's humour. For, though these titles may have been relatively unimportant to him, they were of primary importance to several prominent Soviet composers who held (and sometimes abused) positions of power, in particular the Composers' Union First Secretary Tikhon Khrennikov. Soviet systems of recognition and reward produced a distinct class of powerful bureaucrats, decorated with state honours and given official privileges (better housing, better health care, permission to travel abroad). Shostakovich was himself a member of this class after he joined the Communist Party, since that single act allowed the state to both reward and claim him with positions of considerable material comfort, prestige and responsibility. But his ambivalence, to say the least, towards the pompous behaviour of the Soviet elite is a matter of record. Several friends have revealed anecdotes of Shostakovich launching into hilarious impersonations of these self-important composers and officials; the musicologist Marina Sabinina remembers him lampooning Moscow Conservatoire professors even in the winter of 1949–50 – an exceptionally grim period for Shostakovich:

> A solemn procession trailed past us . . . Dmitri
> Dmitryevich started to imitate their smug, obsequious
> and fawning behaviour, their pompous manners of
> speech. Miming certain of the professors, he played out
> whole scenes, displaying a brilliant gift for comedy in his
> simultaneous impersonations of several characters.[21]

And the composer Krzysztof Meyer recalls him doing something similar on a visit to his home at some time in the 1960s or early '70s. Arriving just after the departure of an official visitor on matters relating to Shostakovich's position as Deputy to the Supreme Soviet, Meyer remembered Shostakovich spending 'nearly half an hour laughing and imitating his salutes, bows and mannerisms'.[22] The conductor Kurt Sanderling, who knew both Shostakovich and Mravinsky very well indeed, has passed on Shostakovich's comment, allegedly made to Mravinsky, that the goose-stepping second movement of the Eighth Symphony depicted 'a functionary granted a business trip abroad'.[23] Deflating pomposity was something Shostakovich had loved to do since his youth, and no doubt holding on to his ability to laugh at the officialdom that so often made his life a misery helped him to cope. The very gentle mockery in his *Preface* is both an acknowledgement that he himself had joined the ranks of Soviet bureaucracy and a preservation of his own self-respect in being able to poke fun at it.

The *Preface* was performed in May 1966, together with his Eleventh Quartet and his song cycles *Five Romances on Texts from Krokodil* (sung by Yevgeny Nesterenko) and *Satires* (sung by Vishnevskaya), both accompanied by Shostakovich. It was his last public appearance as a performer and he suffered badly from nerves, caused both by lack of recent stage experience (it was more than two years since his last public concert) and his awareness that the problems he had recently been suffering with his right hand put his performance in jeopardy. Despite the success of the concert, at which the Eleventh Quartet was encored, the stress of taking part took a swift toll on the composer, who suffered a heart attack upon his return to his hotel room. He barely recovered in time for his sixtieth birthday concert in September 1966, at which Rostropovich premiered his Second Cello Concerto.[24] And it was a long time before he was able to compose again: in January 1967 Shostakovich wrote to Glikman in despair: 'I try to compose something every day, but nothing seems to come of it, and I do not have very high hopes.' A few weeks later he wrote again, apparently in an even darker mood, although his writer's block had ended and he had composed a new song cycle: 'I am . . . disappointed in myself. Or rather, [I have become convinced] that I am a dull, mediocre composer . . . Nevertheless, the urge to compose pursues me like an unhealthy addiction. Today, I finished seven songs to words by Aleksandr Blok.'[25] We learn precisely how he came to finish them from his other friend Veniamin Basner, who remembered that Shostakovich, far from feeling depressed, called him in a thoroughly good mood and asked him to come over and hear his new work. Confessing that when left alone in the house, he had found and consumed a half-bottle of brandy overlooked by Irina (Shostakovich had been forbidden to drink by his doctors and Irina had hidden all the alcohol in their home), Shostakovich felt so invigorated by it that he finished the cycle in just three days. He chose seven poems from early in Blok's career and scored them unconventionally for soprano, piano, violin and cello in various combinations for each song. Despite his extreme stage fright during the May 1966 concert, Shostakovich was still composing piano parts for himself to play at this time, and so, in view of his weakened and unreliable right hand, he scaled back the technical difficulties to a more manageable level.

For all that, the Blok cycle is tough and technically demanding for all the players. Yet it also contains music of great beauty, even nostalgia: 'The City Sleeps' is a wistful evocation of St Petersburg before 1917, where the poet, seeing the far-off glow of dawn reflected in the Neva, seems to prophesy the 'sad days' awaiting him – and perhaps, in Shostakovich's mind, awaiting Blok's fellow Petersburgers as well. The cycle concludes with Blok's untitled poem about music, for which Shostakovich supplied the simple title 'Music': 'At night, when my troubled soul falls asleep/ and the city vanishes in the mist/ oh, how much music there is for God/ what sounds there are in the world!' The following lines could perhaps sum up Shostakovich's own life credo: 'What is the tempest of life to me, when your roses/ flourish and blaze for me?' After eight months of fearing he would never create any more music, as Shostakovich felt the return of his powers these words may have struck a very personal chord.

Shostakovich's fear of drying up was a recurring theme of his later life, having first emerged after Stalin's death in the 1950s and thereafter never entirely leaving him. To Glikman he anxiously cited the examples of Sibelius and Rossini, who both lived for a long time after writing their last significant works. But the self-doubt that went with this anxiety now does seem new: the younger composer never seriously doubted his creative powers and even clung to them as the most important strength he possessed. Perhaps it was his emotional dependence on his identity as a composer that caused him to falter in his self-belief; for if he was not a successful composer, Shostakovich seems to have felt that his life had otherwise been worth very little. The sense that he may have lost a kind of ethical 'calling' also played a part: his decline in moral authority among many of his contemporaries certainly troubled him and he was aware that the trade-off he had privately negotiated between fighting Soviet power and keeping his self-respect, and playing the official parts demanded of him in order to preserve what was left of his mental health and ability to compose, was either misunderstood or rejected as unacceptable by younger colleagues.

Something that strongly characterizes his late music is the fact that it was nearly all composed for specific artists, all friends of Shostakovich, all people who understood his compromised position and did not judge him for it. This was true of his four string concerti, all written for Rostropovich and Oistrakh, as well as for his late quartets, four of them dedicated to a different member of the Beethoven Quartet: the Eleventh to the memory of the second violinist Vasily Shirinsky, the Twelfth to the quartet's leader Dmitry Tsïganov, the Thirteenth to the violist Vadim Borisovsky and the Fourteenth to the cellist Sergey Shirinsky. Shostakovich composed two such 'friendship' works between 1967 and 1968: the Second Violin Concerto, which he completed in May 1967 and dedicated to Oistrakh, and the Twelfth Quartet, completed in March 1968. One of the most approachable and romantic of Shostakovich's late works, the Second Violin Concerto is warmly lyrical, no less so than its predecessor, composed nearly twenty years earlier. The high spirits of its finale emerge, via a long violin solo, from the impassioned climax of the second movement, scored for horn and strings only. In marked contrast with the Second Cello Concerto, the Second Violin Concerto exhibits none of the eccentricities and humour that characterize the work dedicated to Rostropovich, surely a reflection of Shostakovich's understanding of the two musicians' radically different temperaments.

As was immediately noticed, the Twelfth Quartet gestures towards the controversial (because Western and avant-garde) serial technique: a twelve-note theme opens the work but, as though in defiance of the technique's tough image in post-war European and North American serialism, Shostakovich placed it in the context of the most luxuriant of all his string quartet subjects. The second movement posits a similar juxtaposition of twelve-tone writing and assertive diatonicism, opening with a vigorous descending third figure that would, after a long recall of first movement themes, conclude the quartet in a cheerfully robust D flat major. Though in the 1960s many younger Soviet composers would adopt various forms of serial technique, for Shostakovich it had no novelty value at all, since he – unlike the younger composers starved of any 'modern' Western music during their Conservatoire education (even including Shostakovich's early music of the 1920s) – had been aware of twelve-tone music since the 1930s and had rejected it from the start as a viable technique. His very official-sounding statements from the 1960s on the evils of serial composition ('Dodecaphony, serial, pointillist and other kinds of music are one of the greatest evils of twentieth-century music'[26]) may not have been written by him, but he genuinely did regard the technique as overly limiting. However, in a series of works starting with the Blok songs and ending with his Fifteenth Quartet, Shostakovich employed varying forms of twelve-tone technique without, however, ever deviating from his own tonal language. Dmitry Tsïganov, fretting about the possible charge of avant-gardism in the new 'serial' quartet, was firmly told, 'But one finds examples of it in Mozart's music'.[27] Shostakovich was especially pleased with the Twelfth Quartet, perhaps in part because he had so skilfully juggled the famously 'mechanical' technique with such richly expressive music.

His Violin Sonata, a sixtieth birthday gift to Oistrakh, was far less romantic in tone and extremely demanding for both violinist and pianist. Without any hope of being able to accompany Oistrakh himself in public, Shostakovich reverted to his formerly virtuosic piano writing style: the last five or so minutes of the finale contain some of his most challenging piano writing since the First Piano Sonata. He confessed to Glikman that he had accompanied Oistrakh in some rehearsals and found these passages 'awful'.[28] Yet the sonata is not without flashes of humour: in the second movement, the 'trio', a solid B flat major waltz, is plunked down incongruously in the middle of a violent scherzo. Tough and virtuosic, it was a formidable achievement in the midst of constant illness and hospitalization. After breaking his right leg in September 1967 (his left having been broken in 1960 when he fell at Maxim's wedding), Shostakovich reported ironically to Glikman: 'Target achieved so far: 75 per cent (right leg broken, left leg broken, right hand defective').[29] His incapacity meant that he could not attend the premiere of the Second Violin Concerto in September that year, nor the Blok songs in October. Though they could hardly be more different in tone, both the Twelfth Quartet and the Violin Sonata were the fruits of his recovery period in 1968. His next major work, the Fourteenth Symphony, was also conceived and largely written in hospital (in January–February 1969) and addressed the theme that had been in his mind for the last few years: death.

Once again, as with *Stepan Razin*, Shostakovich's spiritual mentor was Musorgsky, specifically his masterpiece *Songs and Dances of Death*. It was above all the terrifying closing song of Musorgsky's cycle, 'The Field Marshal', that inspired the concept behind the new symphony: 'Death is final'. Shostakovich felt so strongly about this message that he actually chose to address the audience before the premiere, a very unusual step for him. Pointing out that composers generally choose to depict death redemptively with 'radiant music', Shostakovich argued against the cliché that 'when you die everything will be fine; what awaits you is absolute peace.'[30] Rather, he asserted, Death ends everything with brutal finality and his aim in the symphony was to protest against this as strongly as possible. Terrified that he would die before completing it, or even hearing it, Shostakovich rated his new symphony as one of his greatest works. To Glikman, he wrote that it 'seems to me a turning point in my work in that everything that I have written for many years now has been in preparation for it'.[31]

The symphony is a cycle of eleven songs, setting poems by Rainer Maria Rilke, Guillaume Apollinaire, Federico García Lorca and the Decembrist and friend of Pushkin Wilhelm Küchelbecker. Each poem depicts death in a different guise: the supernatural ('Lorelei' as well as the prophesy of death in 'On Watch'); the ruined lives after loved ones are taken by war ('Madam! Look'); the living death of jail ('In the Santé Jail'); death by curse ('The Zaporozhian Cossacks' Reply to the Sultan of Constantinople'); a poet's death; the immortality of true friendship after death ('O Delvig'); and finally Rilke's horrifying vision of Death's watchful vigilance: 'Death is all-powerful/ He guards us/ In our hour of joy/ at our greatest moments in life, Death stands watch/ Waits and thirsts/ and laments after us.' Ironically, it was this last song, with its refusal to seek solace in religion, that above all caused offence among some of Shostakovich's contemporaries: yet the message was no more brutal than that delivered by Musorgsky in his own song cycle, above all the 'Serenade', which shows Death greedily awaiting the dying breath of a beautiful young girl, and 'The Field Marshal' where Death, triumphantly surveying the battleground of slaughtered men, declares that he will stamp so heavily on their bones that they will never rise again. For Shostakovich, the finality of death also conveyed a powerful moral message and he said so openly in his introductory words: since there is no afterlife, each human soul must strive to live nobly and die with a clear conscience.

Not since his Thirteenth Symphony had Shostakovich spoken so directly to his fellow citizens. But now any message about morality delivered by the composer risked being thrown back at him. Since the Thirteenth Symphony he, too, had acquired a tarnished reputation: that of complicity by silence. Alexander Solzhenitsyn, a member of the select audience at the premiere, felt angry that Shostakovich had set Apollinaire's 'In the Santé Jail', feeling that it would have been more appropriate to have depicted the living hell of the Gulag (Apollinaire spent only five days in jail). Such anger was symptomatic of Solzhenitsyn's lack of good faith towards the composer by 1969. The previous year Soviet tanks rolled into Prague to crush the 'Prague Spring', causing immense international anger and a demonstration in Red Square at which Flora Litvinova's son Pavel, a prominent figure in the dissident movement, was arrested. Solzhenitsyn, considering collecting signatures of major Soviet cultural figures in protest, changed his mind when he realized none would sign: 'The shackled genius Shostakovich would thrash about like a wounded thing, clasp himself with tightly folded arms so that his fingers could not hold a pen.'[32] One of Shostakovich's favourite quotations was the line spoken by Mozart (and quoted back at the very end by Salieri) in Pushkin's 'Little Tragedy' *Mozart and Salieri*: 'Genius and villainy are incompatible.' Soon those words would be hurled back at him in anger, as his refusal to condemn Soviet crimes became, for some younger contemporaries, an indelible stain on his character.

The Fourteenth Symphony revisits some of the dramatic ideas of his recent work, most notably perhaps the 'freeze-framing' of Lorelei's gaze into the Rhine: like Stepan Razin seeing the boats on the Moscow River reflected in the executioner's axe, Lorelei sees a boat sailing down the river steered by her lover in the moment before her clifftop leap. And in both 'On Watch' and 'Madam! Look' Shostakovich depicted madness as he had never done before. In 'Madam! Look' he achieves this through the over-repetition and disintegration of a simple musical idea in the words 'I laugh', and in 'On Watch' by drawing on the grotesque instrumental effects he had explored in his Second Cello Concerto and Tenth and Eleventh Quartets: eccentrically long string glissandi, here repeated in a kind of frenzy as the protagonist describes the idyllic setting of her furious grief: 'At sunset, the cows are lowing, roses are flaming/ my glance is bewitched by blue birds.' The songs link these techniques – fixation on a simple idea repeated ad nauseam and grotesque use of glissandi – with the idea of madness in a way that reflects intriguingly back upon his use of similar effects in the Tenth and Eleventh Quartets. Genuine sweetness only comes at the end of 'Delvig' where a soft halo of strings gives sanctity to the last line, 'The union of those who love the eternal muse.' For the remorseless concluding words of the symphony, Shostakovich has both soprano and bass declaim together, accompanied by the skeletal sounds of woodblock and castanets ever-insistently 'knocking', a chilling evocation of Death not as a blessed relief from life's burden but as a predatory spectre, eager to claim us.

The symphony was indeed, as Shostakovich had said plainly, a protest: humanity's pain and fear in the face of utter extinction. When asked once if he had any religious faith, Shostakovich responded simply, 'No, and I am very sorry about it.'[33] He was not in any way ready to relinquish life, nor even his health: after completing the symphony, he embarked on a new quest for a cure for his weakened legs and hand, travelling to Siberia to consult with the famous orthopaedic surgeon Dr Gavriil Ilizarov. He stayed in Ilizarov's care for nearly four months and, visited by a reporter in June, seemed a man transformed. After an operation on his right hand, Shostakovich found he was able to play the piano again, practising for up to three hours a day. Although the effects of Ilizarov's treatment did not last long, Shostakovich was by no means ready to give up on his hopes for a cure, returning to Siberia that August and continuing to see Ilizarov regularly over the next few years. That saving characteristic of optimism in his nature, which had been indispensable to him over the course of his difficult life, propelled him forward as he continued to plan and compose new works. At this point in Shostakovich's life, only five years from the end, he still believed he had everything to hope for.

6

Final Years

Although Ilizarov's treatments offered Shostakovich new hope, any improvement in his spirits is hard to detect in his next major work, the Thirteenth Quartet. Another 'friendship' work, dedicated to the Beethoven Quartet's violist Vadim Borisovsky, it is probably the bleakest of the fifteen quartets despite its jazzy middle section, complete with plucked bass and jazz-inflected cross rhythms. It was so dark, in fact, that one young Soviet music critic assumed it was composed in memory of the dedicatee because Borisovsky was no longer a member of the Beethoven Quartet. In fact, though Borisovsky had retired, he was still very much alive; on realizing his error, the mortified critic contacted Shostakovich with fulsome apologies. Fortunately, Shostakovich, whose sense of humour was as keen as ever, seemed more amused than anything else by this very Gogolian slip, which was also an unintentional comment, even an implicit criticism, on how depressing the music was, especially considering it was dedicated to a friend.[1] From a technical perspective, though, the Thirteenth Quartet continued the timbral developments of Shostakovich's late quartet writing, exploring different ways of playing and combining the four instruments. His growing attraction to enigmatic percussion effects, first used by him so long ago at the end of his Fourth Symphony's second movement and revived at the end of the Second Cello Concerto (and thereafter prominent in both the Fourteenth and Fifteenth Symphonies too), now found its way into his quartet writing, with enigmatic taps on the wood of the instruments with the bow adding to the already alienated sound world: yet another instance of *ostranenie* ('making strange') in his late style.

Shostakovich also composed the last of his film music in 1970: an appropriately dark-hued score for Grigory Kozintsev's *King Lear*, which he plundered for the quartet's opening. As refugees from Lear's kingdom appear behind the king, now insane and barely able to recall who he is, a lament for wordless chorus sounds: a keening repetition of a tritone falling to a fourth. The same intervallic shape and falling figure can be heard at the start of the Thirteenth Quartet, resembling the chorus closely enough to identify this as a firm example of film-to-art-music transference (though it also bears a distinct resemblance to the opening of Béla Bartók's *Music for Strings, Percussion and Celesta*).[2] Though always ambivalent about the time and energy spent writing film scores, Shostakovich knew – and said to Flora Litvinova around this time – that much of it was good quality, by no means all hack-work. His late film scores were all written out of long-standing friendship: Lev Arnshtam's biopic *Sofia Perovskaya* (the assassin of Tsar Alexander II) in 1967 and *King Lear* in 1970 rounding off a film career of an astonishing 34 films (not counting Vera Stroyeva's film version of *Khovanshchina*, nor the film versions of *Moscow, Cherëmushki* or *Katerina Izmailova*). He was especially impressed by Kozintsev's two late Shakespeare films, *Hamlet* (1963–4) and *Lear*, and reported to the director that he watched *Hamlet* eight or nine times.[3]

Whether Shostakovich took the same pride in his offering for the centenary celebrations of Lenin's birth in 1970 can only be a matter for conjecture. His choral work *Loyalty* set some truly dreadful poems by his old collaborator Yevgeny Dolmatovsky, which, in their favourable comparison of Lenin to Confucius, Buddha and Allah, achieved new levels of ludicrous flattery. The director of the Taganka Theatre, Yury Lyubimov, remembered how distasteful Shostakovich found these centenary celebrations, declining to attend the special Lenin event Lyubimov had planned despite discussing it enthusiastically with him.[4] If his early letters to Glivenko showed Shostakovich's youthful admiration for Lenin, then that had clearly long since passed, even if he retained sympathy for revolutionary ideals. Yet Dolmatovsky was a friend of Shostakovich, of sorts – their very unequal relationship was never close but it was maintained to the end of Shostakovich's life – and Dolmatovsky had apparently helped Shostakovich gain access to Ilizarov. *Loyalty*'s dedicatee Gustav Ernesaks, the conductor of the Estonian State Academic Male Voice Choir, was not a personal friend but perhaps Shostakovich saw a way of both thanking Dolmatovsky for his recent help and avoiding the pomp of Moscow's Lenin celebrations by writing the work for a choir based in Tallinn. In the end, the Moscow premiere of *Loyalty* did not take place until February 1971, well after the official celebrations had ended.

If *ostranenie* was a major feature of Shostakovich's late style, then with his final symphony, the Fifteenth, he surpassed himself. Here, the young Mitya Shostakovich of the 1920s joins hands with the ageing master and seems both to reassure him that his powers were undimmed and his personality fundamentally unchanged, while also pointing the way forward to the end with a more quizzical, less frightened, gaze. Interpretations of the Fifteenth Symphony abound, as do attempts to decode it by identifying all its quotations and allusions. The matter is complicated even further by Glikman's reporting that Shostakovich himself claimed to quote from Rossini's *William Tell*, Wagner's *Ring* and Beethoven's Sixth Symphony.[5] *William Tell* is the easiest to spot: it jumps cheekily out of the first movement, as though mocking Shostakovich's penchant for anapest rhythms. The finale opens with the *Ring*'s 'Fate' motif first heard in *Die Walküre*, followed by the drumbeat accompanying Siegfried's death in *Götterdämmerung*: so far, all is clear, at least in terms of identifying Shostakovich's sources. But of Beethoven's Sixth Symphony there seems no trace; perhaps

Shostakovich and Oistrakh during rehearsals of the Fifteenth Symphony.

Glikman mis-remembered the Beethoven work Shostakovich named, but no other Beethoven symphony suggests itself as an obvious source either. Some writers have heard an allusion to the 'invasion' theme of the 'Leningrad' Symphony in the double-dotted passacaglia theme of the finale; similarly well established is the idea that, following the *Ring* quotations, Shostakovich feints at the opening of the Prelude from Wagner's *Tristan und Isolde*, only to turn to the Glinka romance 'Do not tempt me needlessly'. So what should we make of these claims and interpretations? The benefit of hindsight, knowing this was Shostakovich's last symphony, makes the wish to decode these quotations and find further allusions to earlier Shostakovich works especially tempting, but it is a mistake to expect a work that draws its energies precisely from those enigmatic qualities to give up its secrets. The quotations and allusions entice us in, inviting us to interpret but never relinquish a single answer.

The *Ring* quotations are incontrovertible, and the stringing-out of the *Tristan* motif's opening gesture underlines Shostakovich's love of juxtaposing the serious and the comic, or at least the gently humorous. As soon as we hear Wagner's voice – the great harbinger of doom, a magisterial presence in Leningrad's concert halls (and opera houses) throughout the pre-war years – Shostakovich teases us, knowing the instantaneous aural connection will be made and audiences will expect the inevitable 'Tristan chord'. Yet though Glinka's song begins with an identical four-note shape, the way that Shostakovich develops his own theme, allowing it to become gently dance-like before pausing and turning back on itself, bears no resemblance at all to 'Do not tempt me needlessly'. In all likelihood, this song was not even in Shostakovich's mind as he wrote the symphony. The point was surely always to tease and puncture the Wagnerian pretensions of the finale's opening: a classic piece of Shostakovich self-mockery. But what of the 'Leningrad' quotation: is this any more promising? Again, the resemblance between the finale's passacaglia theme and the invasion theme of the Seventh Symphony is weak: though the intervallic shapes are similar, the change in metre is fundamental: the Fifteenth Symphony's triple metre lends it a totally different character. In any case it would be rash to conclude that such an allusion – even if it is there at all – was deliberate, or meant anything specific. In conversation with Glikman, Shostakovich maintained that he did not really know why any of the quotations were there at all – but he 'could *not*, could *not*, *not* include them'.[6] Glikman's suggestion that the allusions may have been simply intuitive – to which Shostakovich replied 'Maybe' – seems eminently plausible.

The conductor Kurt Sanderling, who had known Shostakovich since the 1930s when he worked as Mravinsky's assistant in the Leningrad Philharmonia, found the Fifteenth by far Shostakovich's bleakest symphony. In 1996 he asserted, 'no other work of his [is] as radically horrible and cruel as the Fifteenth Symphony.

It's a horrific work about loneliness and death.'[7] The horror, it seems, is inescapably in the ear of the listener. Certainly, the first movement's mercurial temperament suggests nothing so strongly as Stravinsky's *Petrushka*: donning one playful mask after the other, and in that sense harking right back to the opening of Shostakovich's First Symphony, which is similarly *Petrushka*-like. And a further link with the First Symphony is found in the funeral march of the second movement: if in the First Symphony Shostakovich had his dying friend Volodya Kurchavov in mind, in the Fifteenth he may have been contemplating his own end. Towards the end of the movement Shostakovich seems to allude to the 'Elmira' horn calls of the Tenth Symphony's third movement: though he does not evoke it openly by scoring it for horn solo, a version of the call is heard instead on low strings at the end of the movement, before the funeral chorale brings it to a sombre conclusion. Then abruptly plunging us back into the world of the 1920s, the scherzo's grotesque-playful opening theme is pure early Shostakovich, while the middle section again evokes Stravinsky, this time the jolly-but-creepy march of *L'Histoire du soldat*. A piquant blend of the sinister, the comic and the genial, the scherzo is constantly shape-shifting, trying on different personalities for size, as though Shostakovich was revisiting his Leningrad youth and meeting ghosts around every corner.

The death-haunted finale takes us back to the older, greyer world of the 1970s. Yet though 'desolate', 'lonely' and 'tragic' are all adjectives commonly encountered when reading about this movement, we might consider the possibility that its ending is more hopeful than despairing; or at least that it contemplates death in a very different light to that found in the Fourteenth Symphony. While the passacaglia theme echoes in the bass, Shostakovich concludes his symphonic cycle by reaching into a world beyond: shadowy, alien, but not sinister, even strangely peaceful. Returning again to the magical percussion effects of the Fourth Symphony and Second Cello Concerto, he uses celesta, piccolo and triangle as his 'magic bells' evoking another realm, whether that of the enchanted garden in *Ruslan and Lyudmila* or Sarastro's temple in *The Magic Flute*. Shostakovich's own reaction after the premiere was not remotely one of distress, overcome with emotion. What he said was, 'I think I've written a wicked symphony.'[8] The Russian term he used, *likhoy*, means both 'evil' and 'dashing'; the nearest English equivalent is the colloquial term 'wicked' to mean 'excellent', or perhaps also 'awesome'. It was intended to baffle, intended to poke fun, but also perhaps intended to join up both ends of his career. Beset by fears but also able to transcend them, the composer of the Fifteenth Symphony was entirely the match of his younger self.

Sadly, soon after finishing the Fifteenth Symphony Shostakovich suffered another heart attack and was forced to endure another protracted hospital stay, this time for two months. Yet even on return home Shostakovich composed nothing at all for a year, making this creative hiatus the longest he had ever experienced. There were clear health reasons for much of it: in December 1972 he was diagnosed with lung cancer and stayed in hospital for radiation treatment until February 1973. Foreign trips also invaded what might have been his habitual creative windows of opportunity, taking up his time and energy in the summer and autumn of 1972. There were trips to Berlin, London, Aldeburgh, York and Dublin (for another honorary doctorate), all squeezed in between leaving hospital after his heart attack and going back there for his cancer treatment. Physically Shostakovich had never been at such a low ebb. No wonder that he wrote in despair to Glikman in January 1973,

> I have almost forgotten what it is like to be at home . . .
> I have lost [my health] and am wretched because of it. I
> am almost completely helpless in the ordinary business
> of life; I can no longer do things like dress myself or wash

myself on my own. Some kind of spring has broken in
my brain. I have not written a note since the Fifteenth
Symphony. This is a terrible state of affairs for me.[9]

Another cause of sorrow was the deaths of many of his dearest
contemporaries: the dedicatee of his last quartet, Vadim Borisovsky,
died in 1972 and in 1973 Shostakovich lost his beloved sister Maria
as well as his old friends Levon Atovmyan and Grigory Kozintsev.

Yet even in this year of illness and loss (1972) Shostakovich was
planning a new opera, this time on Chekhov's powerful short story
'The Black Monk'. It is easy to understand Shostakovich's attraction
to this story, which he had loved since his youth: its interweaving of
genius, inspiration and madness conveyed an unsettling message
that would have been only too close to his heart. Chekhov shows a
brilliant young man driven mad by an apparition (the black monk),
but while mad, he was happy and productive in his career. Once
his loved ones realize his mental state, they take him for treatment;
he ceases to see the black monk but descends into utter misery. In
the end, furious with them for destroying the exalted happiness
his madness gave him, he rejects family life completely and only
regains happiness in the moment before his death when he sees the
apparition one last time. Shostakovich had always paid a high price
for his brilliance: it had given him a successful career and perhaps
secured his immortality too (a theme he would revisit soon in his
Michelangelo songs), but it had also caused him untold misery.
That he should have begun thinking about the story again at this
particular point in his life is also suggestive, because during any
period of creative block Shostakovich was intensely unhappy. His
friends found him most cheerful just after completing a major work:
though other aspects of life gave him pleasure, he was only really
happy when composing, as though without it his life lacked any
purpose. Without his composing, indeed, he was just a sick elderly
man, nursed and cared for lovingly, but helplessly dependent and

stripped of his formerly precious dignity and privacy. Perhaps, like Chekhov's protagonist Kovrin, Shostakovich had long ago decided he was willing to pay whatever price was required in order to serve his muse. In the words of his final Blok setting, addressed to music: 'Accept, Sovereign mistress/ through blood, torment and the grave/ this last cup of passion/ from your unworthy slave!'

In a last-ditch attempt to rekindle his creative spark, Shostakovich decided to ignore his doctors' advice and resume drinking. Soon he had revived sufficiently to start composing again and in the space of a month had completed his Fourteenth Quartet, the last of his dedications to his old friends the Beethoven Quartet. The new work was dedicated to the cellist Sergey Shirinsky, and Shostakovich affectionately wove in a tribute to Shirinsky by way of quoting Katerina's line to Sergey in *Lady Macbeth*: 'Serëzha, my darling' (final movement, starting at bar 146 on cello). That he could recall this moment now as a tribute to Shirinsky speaks volumes about the different emotional world Shostakovich was inhabiting since he quoted the same passage in the Eighth Quartet. In fact, the Fourteenth Quartet could lay a plausible claim to being Shostakovich's most radiant work: cast in his 'love music' key of F sharp major (a trope established long ago in his opera *Lady Macbeth*), the genial first movement gives way to a slow movement that is tenderly lyrical rather than overcast. Shostakovich was especially pleased with the sentimental cello melody at fig. 52, which he called his 'Italian bit' and reprised (this time for violin) in the coda. The quartet's ending achieves a serenity almost unique in Shostakovich's entire output: the gentle F sharp major cadences are both sincere and hard-won. Right at the end of Shostakovich's life, he was finally able to express peace in his music.

Shostakovich only completed one more work in 1973: his *Six Verses by Marina Tsvetaeva*, written on holiday in Estonia in early August 1973. The poems he chose all focus in different ways on the three themes that continually recurred in Shostakovich's song settings: love, the creative spirit and its relation to power. In 'Hamlet's Dialogue with his Conscience', Tsvetaeva and Shostakovich sternly address Hamlet's glaring deficiency with regard to Ophelia in the light of his hypocritical protestations of love at her burial site; in the next two poems, 'Poet and Tsar' and 'No, the Drum did Beat', Tsvetaeva points an accusing finger at Tsar Nicholas I, the 'poet-killer', for his humiliation of Pushkin, while in 'No, the Drum did Beat' she raises the spectacle, which Shostakovich must have begun contemplating with regard to himself, of the poet's funeral attended by so many functionaries that his closest friends could barely find a space to grieve. Dripping sarcasm from every bar, Shostakovich must have relished setting the words, 'Behold, my country, see how, contrary to opinion/the Monarch cares for a poet!' Finally, Tsvetaeva's tribute to Anna Akhmatova ('O Muse of tears, loveliest of all Muses') gave Shostakovich the opportunity to repay the homage Akhmatova had paid him during their careers. What Shostakovich had been in music, Akhmatova had been in poetry: they were similar ages, similarly revered internationally as well as at home, and had each suffered both direct and indirect persecution. Akhmatova, like Shostakovich, had been treated brutally during the post-war *Zhdanovshchina* and had lost both husband and, in a different way (emotionally rather than physically), her son to different periods of political terror. She dedicated her own poem, 'Music', to Shostakovich, 'in whose epoch I lived on earth'. Shostakovich's final setting is both a tribute to his contemporary and to his much-missed city of Leningrad ('I give you my city of bell-towers').

After completing the cycle, events affecting Shostakovich's personal relationships deteriorated rapidly, putting paid to the peace of mind he had seemingly achieved with the Fifteenth Symphony and the Fourteenth Quartet. For in August 1973 *Pravda* published a full-scale attack on the Nobel Prize-winning nuclear physicist Andrey Sakharov and a few days later an open letter to the paper, entitled 'A Disgrace to the Name of Citizen', was published, signed by twelve distinguished Soviet musicians. Shostakovich's name was among the signatories. The fallout was devastating for the composer, especially in his weakened and fragile state: he had been told by American doctors a few months earlier that he was terminally ill. Irina Shostakovich maintained in 2000 that Shostakovich did not in fact sign the letter, and that they deliberately spent the entire day away from home in order to avoid being asked to sign. In the end, she asserts, Shostakovich's signature was simply added without his consent.[10] Whether he told anyone that he had not signed is uncertain: it seems not, since no one else defended him this way, either before or after his death, but perhaps Shostakovich felt that either he would not be believed and so trying to defend himself would simply sound childish (and being disbelieved by friends would have been even more painful), or he may have feared that allowing such a rumour to spread might be dangerous. What happened next, in September 1973, must have been deeply hurtful to him. The human rights activist and dissident Lidia Chukovskaya, daughter of the Soviet writer Korney Chukovsky, wrote an open letter in defence of Sakharov, and added the following line: 'Shostakovich's signature on the protest of musicians against Sakharov demonstrates irrefutably that the Pushkinian question has been resolved forever: genius and villainy are compatible.'[11] Since Pushkin's statement (spoken by Mozart, and then echoed as a question by Salieri) that they were *not* compatible was a maxim that Shostakovich himself liked to quote, those words would have hit home. He had preached moral and personal ethics to fellow citizens in his Thirteenth and Fourteenth Symphonies (at least in his introductory talk for the Fourteenth) and to now be publicly accused of breaching his own ethical standards was humiliating, all the more so because there was nothing at all he could do but take the consequences.

The most painful episode in the aftermath was described by Edison Denisov, who himself felt angry with his friend and mentor. But when he witnessed the frail composer struggling to his feet to shake Yury Lyubimov's hand, only for the theatre director to cut him dead, he called Lyubimov to task. But Lyubimov simply replied, 'After Shostakovich signed that letter against Sakharov I can't shake his hand.'[12] Many people, Denisov recalled, felt the same way. Shostakovich even received hostile letters as well as enduring these unfriendly encounters. What made it worse was that Rostropovich was himself becoming an active dissident, and Shostakovich feared for his friend when he saw him wholeheartedly supporting not only Sakharov but Solzhenitsyn, as the writer found himself increasingly *persona non grata*. He was stripped of his citizenship and expelled from the Soviet Union in February 1974 and, to Shostakovich's immense distress, Rostropovich followed him in May, ostensibly for a two-year period in order to allow him to pursue his career normally, since playing opportunities were being curtailed at home due to his political support for dissidents. Vishnevskaya and their two daughters departed two months later; Shostakovich would never see any of them again. When Rostropovich braced himself to tell Shostakovich the news, the composer immediately began weeping, asking pitifully 'In whose hands are you leaving me to die?'[13] The regime that Shostakovich was forced to publicly support was now responsible for driving away one of his dearest friends, leaving him more isolated than ever.

Yet somehow he managed to carry on writing music. That summer he was extraordinarily productive, completing his next (and final) quartet, the Fifteenth, and two song cycles, the *Suite on Texts of Michelangelo Buonarroti* and *Four Verses of Captain Lebyadkin*, drawn from Dostoevsky's novel (a long-standing favourite of Shostakovich's) *The Devils*. As he had done so often before, Shostakovich used composing as a way of working through personal grief: the Fifteenth Quartet contains some of the most melancholy music he ever wrote. Its unusual structure – six Adagios running seamlessly together – sets it apart from his more recent quartets, as does the fact that it carries no dedication. The first movement, 'Elegy', is infused with quiet sadness; the second theme, at fig. 6, reaches for the light in a suddenly hopeful C major, but this is snuffed out by the movement's end, back in the quartet's home key of E flat minor. A sinister 'Serenade' follows, with violent pizzicato chords and aggressively squeezed crescendi evoking rage and frustration, followed by an 'Intermezzo', a 'Nocturne' and a 'Funeral March'. The sixth and final movement, 'Epilogue', does offer a kind of resolution when the first movement's theme returns transformed into E flat major, though this moment of brightness quickly passes; at fig. 70 Shostakovich quotes from the first movement of his Sixth Symphony (clarinet duet, figs. 20–21), allowing this prominent dotted theme to fuse with that of the funeral march of the quartet; at fig. 73 he recalls the 'Nocturne' viola melody, but the shrouding blanket of demi-semiquavers stifles its lyrical voice. Quietly and in a mood of intense foreboding, the funeral march figure brings the Fifteenth Quartet to a hushed close. Planned as usual to be premiered by the Beethoven Quartet, now without both its original second violinist and its violist, who had both died, the quartet rehearsed for Shostakovich on the morning of 18 October; later that very same day Sergey Shirinsky, the cellist and dedicatee of the Fourteenth Quartet, passed away. Fearful that he, too, might die before hearing his quartet performed, Shostakovich asked the Leningrad-based Taneyev Quartet to give the premiere; he was well enough to travel to Leningrad that November and attend the concert.

His next work, the Michelangelo cycle, was the closest that the atheist Shostakovich ever came to a religious work. Reading a translation of Michelangelo's poetry in 1974, he picked eleven verses, all on major human themes: love, death, immortality, art,

Shostakovich and Irina after the premiere of the Fifteenth Quartet.

truth. But he also set poems dealing with political persecution in the two songs about Dante Alighieri: the first, simply entitled 'Dante' and the second 'To the Exile'. In 'Night', too, the poet reflects that his beautiful statue would prefer to 'sleep' rather than be awakened 'when all around is shame and infamy'. As with the earlier cycle *Satires*, these poems were chosen for their obvious political relevance, but, unlike the *Satires*, here Shostakovich is in deadly earnest. In 'To the Exile', which Irina Shostakovich claimed was written with Solzhenitsyn in mind, at the words 'But, while heaven opened to him its door/ His homeland viciously locked the door on him', Shostakovich recreates the 'freeze-frame' sound world of the moments before Stepan Razin's murder and preceding Lorelei's leap into the Rhine. Dante's contemporaries, the poet states, were 'blinded by his greatness' and so exiled him. Dante's link with Razin and Lorelei is clear: they were all destroyed by those in power who could not bear to see the light they shone on

Shostakovich and the Taneyev Quartet during rehearsal.

those around them. The pain and anger in the music that follows this moment is the most eloquent protest Shostakovich could have made against Solzhenitsyn's treatment. If anything, 'Death' is even more pointed: 'There is no hope, and darkness covers all/ And lies prevail, Truth casting down its glance'. When his earlier cycle *Satires* was performed, the most politically suggestive of Chërny's verses, 'Our Posterity' meant the cycle could not be broadcast on Soviet television unless the performers (Rostropovich and Vishnevskaya) agreed to omit it, which they did not. These official sensitivities were telling in a way that was both ironically funny and oppressive: a poem clearly applying to pre-revolutionary times could be considered seditious by officials who saw only too clearly the imperfections of the regime for which they themselves were cultural watchdogs. Yet by 1974, though the cultural climate was far more oppressive, Shostakovich was considered such a safe proposition that these transparently accusatory verses barely raised an official eyebrow. What made them even safer was that Shostakovich had explained that he was setting Michelangelo's poems in tribute to the forthcoming five-hundred-year centenary celebrations; it would not be feasible to ban the poems of a major cultural icon on the brink of his 500th birthday. And so it was here, through these powerful verses written half a millennium ago, that Shostakovich was able to give vent to his anger and sadness, not just through the medium of a string quartet but with words to make his feelings absolutely clear.

In other respects too, though, the Michelangelo songs rank among Shostakovich's most important late works. The way in which he chose to set the texts can feel counter-intuitive: all three of the love poems, 'Morning', 'Love' and 'Separation', strike a much more serious note than we might have expected, given the words. 'Morning' in particular could seem slightly cheeky: the lover regards his beloved in full dress and considers the delicious anticipation of disrobing her again: to the sash around her waist that seems to whisper 'I'll never part from her', the poet responds, 'O, how much work there is for my hands to do here!' Shostakovich's sombre tone takes us from the world of a sixteenth-century young poet to the perspective of a much older man, for whom the desired object of love is almost too sacred to be touched. All the 'love' songs are serious in tone, but they are also tender, without a shred of playfulness. Only in the final song, 'Immortality', does Shostakovich's lighter-hearted tone reappear, and it does so in a way that is all the more moving for being so unexpected. The text alone leads us to anticipate a dark, valedictory song:

So Fate has granted me untimely sleep/ But I am not dead, though buried in the ground/ I live in you, whose laments I can hear/ Because friends are reflected in each other. I seem to be dead, but, as comfort to the world/ I live as a thousand souls in the hearts/ Of all those who love me; therefore, I am not dust/ And deathly decay cannot touch me.

But instead of a melancholy setting, we hear a sweet-natured, piping melody for clarinet, flute and piccolo, reprised at the end of the first verse. A much more serious note sounds in the second verse: anticipating his own imminent death, and knowing that his loved ones will grieve, Shostakovich speaks both to their sadness and to his own longing to go on living through his music. Though the opening melody is not repeated at the end, we hear the same harmonies on strings, as though accompanying the tune that is no longer there, thus signalling the presence of this gentle spirit even in its absence. The return of this childlike, innocent voice – in abeyance since the Thirteenth Symphony's finale – is one of the most moving passages in all of Shostakovich's late music. Shostakovich never actually heard his own scoring of the songs: like nearly all his song cycles, it was composed for voice and piano, and scored soon afterwards. He was especially pleased with the interpretation given by the original pianist, Yevgeny Shenderovich; but it is only through Shostakovich's orchestration that we can fully appreciate the connections between 'Night' and the fates of Stepan Razin and Lorelei. And the instruments he chose to represent his own immortality – high wind, with a quirky, slightly grotesque celesta figure rounding things off – confirm more eloquently than is possible in the piano part the youthful spirit he identified with. Indeed, he confessed after a performance to colleagues that he had composed this theme in his youth, but had never been able to use it until now.[14] It is the only moment of serenity, even happiness, in this serious, deeply felt cycle.

Shostakovich's penultimate work is one very rarely performed, and his literary source was as unconventional as Gogol's 'The Nose' had been for an opera. In Dostoevsky's novel *The Devils*, alongside the truly evil characters of Pëtr Verkhovensky and the equally depraved Nikolay Stavrogin, the ridiculous Captain Lebyadkin appears: an amoral blackmailer and drunkard. His attempts to write and recite his poetry are laughable, but are also intended to be uncomfortable: he is a buffoon, but a dangerous and unpleasant one. Shostakovich remarked to Glikman, 'The character of Captain Lebyadkin has something of the buffoon, but there is also something that is much more sinister about him.'[15] Shostakovich set not only his 'poems', but his introductory and explanatory words, and the titles as well, underlining their absurd nature. There is more than a hint here of the long-extinguished 'absurdist' school of Russian poetry exemplified by Daniil Kharms, and much loved by Shostakovich in his youth. The first song, ironically entitled 'Love', sets three such absurd offerings, with titles including 'To the Perfection of Mademoiselle Tushina' and 'Supposing She Breaks her Leg', a rumination on how, when the 'Beauty of Beauties broke her Member', her admirer fell twice as deeply in love with her. To underline the futility of Lebyadkin's admiration, Shostakovich cruelly inserts the opening line of Yeletsky's forlorn aria, 'I love you', to Liza in Tchaikovsky's *Queen of Spades*. Yeletsky, sensing that Liza (his betrothed) no longer loves him, can do no more than lay his soul bare to the woman slipping from his grasp. It is in fact a truly poignant moment in the opera, since Liza will leave the honest Yeletsky for the deranged Hermann, an act that leads to her own suicide. Shostakovich's quotation is thus doubly provocative, mocking not only the thoroughly degraded Lebyadkin, but Yeletsky, the only noble male character in Tchaikovsky's opera. The final song, 'A Luminous Personality', sets Lebyadkin's loutish toast to a Russian revolutionary student: 'Everyone waits for him/Will follow him unswervingly/ To wipe out the ruling class/ And the Tsars as well/ To render all property common/ and to forever take revenge/ On the church, marriage and family/ Those crimes of the old regime! Ekh!' Though Dostoevsky wrote those words in 1871–2, how prescient they proved to be: Shostakovich, again sailing close to the wind, realized their full satirical potential, with a vengeance. What Lebyadkin admires is not the best of revolutionary ideals, but their worst, taken to absurd levels. And what both Dostoevsky and Shostakovich show is that Lebyadkin was not a one-off idiot, but merely an ignorant, malignant thug of the type that enabled the worst excesses of the Soviet regime. It must have afforded Shostakovich intense satisfaction to produce these songs right at the end of his career – and at the same time show that, in the works of great writers like Michelangelo and Dostoevsky, the same themes recur time and again: power and its abuse is as eternal a theme as love and death.

As well as his long-standing admiration for Dostoevsky, Shostakovich had never forgotten his old love of Gogol – he re-read him over and over again and could recite long passages by heart. But he received a powerful incentive to revisit his older satirical style when in 1972 Boris Pokrovsky, director of the Moscow Chamber Music Theatre, suggested reviving his opera *The Nose*. Even though the opera had never been performed again in the Soviet Union, Shostakovich had had the chance to hear it comparatively recently, since earlier revivals had taken place in various European cities in the 1960s, and Shostakovich had played a recording of one of these (the Deutsche Staatsoper production from 1969) to his friends. Pokrovsky finally secured the Soviet revival performance, with Gennady Rozhdestvensky conducting, in 1974. Seeing it was a moment of pure joy for Shostakovich; the film made of the very same production in 1979 shows a glimpse of the composer from the (also filmed) 1974 production right at the beginning. He attended rehearsals when well enough to come, and Pokrovsky, who of course saw the original filmed production, remembered that when the camera showed Shostakovich's face during the Summer Gardens episode, the composer was seen to be mouthing the words and reacting with spontaneous pleasure to what he heard and saw. In this revival, as well as in his Lebyadkin and Michelangelo songs, there is a sense of a wheel coming full circle: the gaze back to his Leningrad youth, before the horrors of the Stalin regime fully revealed themselves, began with his

Fifteenth Symphony and would end only in his very last work, the Viola Sonata, written for Fëdor Druzhinin, Vadim Borisovsky's replacement in the Beethoven Quartet.

Perhaps it was his re-acquaintance with *The Nose* that piqued Shostakovich's interest in his other lost Gogol project, *The Gamblers*. In 1974 Shostakovich asked Galina Ustvolskaya to return his manuscript score of the opera to him, having given it to her many years earlier. And so in the space of just a few months Shostakovich not only watched his beloved opera *The Nose* performed (in a fantastic staging) for the first time on Russian soil since 1930, but also sat down with *The Gamblers* and reminded himself how much good music there was in the score, which was in imminent danger of falling into complete obscurity. And so, when he turned to his next work, the Viola Sonata, Shostakovich decided to rescue it. The second movement of the sonata follows the opera from its very first page with absolute precision, including vocal parts, for more than two minutes, covering the brief minute-long orchestral introduction and the first minute or so of the text, where the main character Ikharev and his servant Alexey settle down in the country inn where the action will take place. Again, the old Shostakovich is consciously reconnecting with his younger self, relishing his music's spiky energy. But it is the finale where he does something quite unique: he quotes the opening bars – in some cases just a single bar – of every single one of his symphonies (the Eleventh is the only exception, as here it comes from the second movement) in rapid succession. Yet this cycle of self-quotations is almost impossible to hear, even when you know what to listen for: they are not supposed to be heard, but are subtly embedded in both viola and (for the last three quotations) deep in the piano's lowest register. They have been found and identified thanks to the detective work of the pianist and composer Ivan Sokolov, with added assistance from Shostakovich's friend Krzysztof Meyer.[16]

Alongside these near-inaudible quotations, however, there is another major theme in the finale that *is* clearly audible, and that is the dramatic descending theme from the opening of Shostakovich's very first publicly performed and published work: his Suite for Two Pianos, which he and his sister Maria had performed in the prestigious Circle of the Friends of New Music concert in Petrograd, 22 June 1923. It is possible that Shostakovich began the Viola Sonata on or around that date in 1975, since we know that it was in late June that he informed Fëdor Druzhinin that he was going to write it and wanted to consult with him on technical questions. Since Shostakovich had completed the first two movements by 4 July, the date of their 'technical' phone conversation when he wanted to check details of the finale, it is almost certain that he conceived the idea of reusing the Suite's dramatic opening theme from very early on. With his penchant for remembering important dates, especially of first performances very early in his career, it is highly probable that Shostakovich remembered the date of 22 June as his first significant public appearance as a composer and it is very tempting to imagine that it was the combination of the auspicious date, the memory of his father's death when he felt his own was imminent, and his wish to commemorate his career through these half-concealed quotations, that brought the Suite's theme so prominently into his mind. Alongside this dramatic falling figure, the most obvious musical influence on the finale is that of Beethoven's 'Moonlight' Sonata (first movement), woven into the piano's slow broken chords accompanying the viola's dotted rhythm. Shostakovich told Druzhinin that the finale was an adagio in memory of Beethoven, but impressed on him that the sonata was not funereal but 'bright and clear': it is certainly valedictory, but never bleak or depressing. Its warm C major ending echoes that of Mahler's *Das Lied von der Erde*, the work which Shostakovich had often said he would choose to listen to if he had only an hour left to live. Right at the end of his life Shostakovich did not want

Shostakovich in June 1975.

to dwell on painful memories; he wanted to bid a loving farewell to all that he held dear. Writing to Druzhinin from hospital, Shostakovich told him the score would be ready at the beginning of August; he managed to return home very briefly, but on 4 August was taken back into hospital after suffering seizures. The lung cancer he had known about since 1972 was now affecting his other organs. Though Druzhinin started rehearsing the sonata promptly after collecting it from Irina on 6 August, hoping to play it to Shostakovich as soon as he was out of hospital again, Shostakovich died in the evening of 9 August. His Viola Sonata was the only completed work of his that he never heard performed.

Druzhinin and his pianist Mikhail Muntian gave the premiere of the sonata first privately in his home on what would have been Shostakovich's 69th birthday. Then on 1 October they gave the formal premiere in the Glinka Hall (the chamber music hall) of the Leningrad Philharmonia. Druzhinin recalled in his memoir that the small hall was so crowded the adjoining doors to the

Shostakovich's grave at Novodevichy Cemetery.

concert hall had to be opened because otherwise the audience overflowed into the foyer. What would have been Shostakovich's place at the concert was left empty but for flowers. During the concert Druzhinin's wife sat next to Yevgeny Mravinsky, who had worked closely with Shostakovich since the momentous premiere of his Fifth Symphony in December 1937. During the concert, she told her husband, Mravinsky wept unceasingly and by the end he was shaking with sobs. In Druzhinin's own words, 'To speak of the sonata being a success would simply have been improper. What happened that night . . . was something greater than music.'[17] The Soviet Union had lost its greatest composer, that much was obvious; but many at the concert had also lost a cherished friend and comrade. That Russian audiences would never again see their beloved Shostakovich, no matter how elderly or infirm, was an unbearably painful reality. The inevitable state funeral took place as the composer himself had predicted in his Tsvetaeva setting; but there were some personal requests honoured too. Shostakovich was buried next to his first wife Nina, as he had wanted, in the Novodevichy Convent cemetery in Moscow. A simple granite headstone reads 'Dmitri Dmitrievich Shostakovich 1906–1975', with the DSCH motif surrounded by a laurel wreath. Like Gustav Mahler's grave, Shostakovich's makes no mention of his profession. In Mahler's own words, 'any who come to look for me will know who I was and the rest don't need to know'.[18]

Postlude

Dmitry Shostakovich's life was one of constant accommodation: first with malnutrition and poverty, then with a rapidly changing political climate, restrictions on his career, personal terror and anguish, and ultimately with the necessity of serving the regime who had wrought all these things. That he not only managed to preserve his calling as a composer, but rarely even slightly deviated from his own high professional standards, was something that very few other contemporary Soviet creative artists achieved. The poet Anna Akhmatova was one of the few like him who had not only the talent but the personal qualities that somehow enabled her to endure a life of very similar (if anything, more severe) emotional stress while jealously guarding her own voice. But what were those qualities? In his darker moments Shostakovich was not under any illusions about his own instinct for survival. After the Sakharov incident he compared himself unflatteringly to Chekhov's morally bankrupt Dr Ragin from 'Ward No. 6', who persuades himself, little by little, to accommodate all the negative aspects of his hospital and his patients' treatment until he no longer sees them. In such a half-alive state he is considered a successful professional. But when he befriends a patient and his conscience slowly begins to awaken, those around him come to regard him as similarly deranged, and he ends up being confined in his own brutal asylum, beaten by the guard who used to respect him.

Was Shostakovich really like Dr Ragin? Those who loved him would have protested vigorously against such a negative portrait. Yet it is wishful thinking to imagine that he could have been as successful as he was within the Soviet system without some Ragin-like reserves of pragmatism and instinct for self-preservation. As Chekhov shows, once this armour begins to crumble, destruction swiftly follows. Shostakovich could not afford the luxury of publicly condemning Stalin's crimes any more than any other Soviet citizen of those years could. But he did maintain at least the aim of living by the principles he had been brought up with. During his career he performed many acts of extreme generosity and courage, many of which we probably do not even know about. It is sheer good luck, for instance, that the composer Isaak Schwarz discovered that Shostakovich had been secretly paying for his Conservatoire education.[1] Following Stalin's death, Shostakovich petitioned Beria repeatedly for the release of the composer Alexander Veprik; and we have already seen how he interceded for Weinberg, even when Stalin was still alive. Given the post-1948 climate of anti-Semitism, driven by Stalin's paranoia and growing obsession with Jews, these were acts of immense courage. He did for others what Gorky and Tukhachevsky had done for him in 1936: used his professional status as a shield with which to protect others who were more vulnerable.

However, there is no doubt that, in particular after joining the Communist Party, Shostakovich seemed to divide himself into compartments, one of which was his official face, smiling and even kissing (a standard Russian greeting: three times on the cheeks) politicians and senior colleagues whom he did not actually like. Irina Shostakovich told the journalist and writer Martin Sixsmith something of the real relationship between Shostakovich and Tikhon Khrennikov, the powerful First Secretary of the Composers' Union of the USSR:

Khrennikov is old now, but he's still up to his old tricks. I remember when Dmitri criticized one of his compositions. He flew into a rage and wrote some awful attack on Dmitri. He hated Dmitri for the rest of his life. Outwardly, they both pretended they got on well with each other. They had to . . . Dmitri used to say: 'If it wasn't Khrennikov, someone else would have done it . . . maybe someone even worse'.[2]

Shostakovich had personally survived the Stalin purges, but lost many dear friends and his peace of mind would never wholly return. He did not want to engage in angry polemics with people who could make miserable not only his own life, but those of his students, his family (Maxim's career as a conductor was just getting started in the last decade or so of Shostakovich's life) and potentially other people around him too. This was pure self-preservation, a pragmatic response to past trauma. Judging him for this – especially from a comfortable perspective that has never experienced political terror – is, to my mind at least, not an option. Dr Ragin never had to deal with a legacy like that of Shostakovich.

But if we cannot judge him for his reluctant complicity, we also cannot seek to elevate him above his fellow citizens as a heroic resister of communism, as Solomon Volkov and some other post-*Testimony* commentators sought to do. Many others, especially from the 1960s onward, paid dearly for their resistance to the Communist regime, while Shostakovich lived the privileged life of the Soviet elite. What is more, Shostakovich would, I am convinced, have found the suggestion that he was in any way heroic extremely distasteful. To airbrush out the inconvenient facts in order to create our own vision of a dissident, a hero, a man who was more moral than anyone else, is simply to replace the historical reality with a mirage. It does no honour to Shostakovich's memory to see him this way – a one-dimensional resistor to Soviet power. If that is all we see, we fail to acknowledge the sheer torture of his divided existence. The more directly we look into his face, the better we understand both his troubled times and his music.

References

Prelude: Writing About Shostakovich

1 Solomon Volkov, *Testimony: The Memoirs of Dmitri Shostakovich*, as relayed to and ed. Solomon Volkov, trans. Antonina W. Bouis (New York, 1979).
2 See chiefly Laurel Fay, 'Shostakovich versus Volkov: Whose *Testimony*?' and 'Volkov's *Testimony* Reconsidered', in *A Shostakovich Casebook*, ed. Malcolm Hamrick Brown (Bloomington, IN, 2004), pp. 11–66. See also the following 'A Side-by-side Comparison of Texts from *Testimony* with their Original Sources', ibid., pp. 69–79.

1 'She did not wait for me'

1 Rosa Sadykhova, 'Letters to this Mother, 1923–1927', trans. Rolanda Norton, in *Shostakovich and his World*, ed. Laurel Fay (Princeton, NJ, 2004), p. 5.
2 Ol'ga Digonskaya, 'Yavorskiy', in *Shostakovich v Leningradskoy Konservatorii, 1919–1930*, ed. Lyudmila Kovnatskaya, Anna Petrova, Lidia Ader and Pavel Gershenzon, (St Petersburg, 2013), vol. II, p. 98.
3 Elizabeth Wilson, *Shostakovich: A Life Remembered*, rev. edn (London, 2006), p. 52.
4 Ibid., p. 63.
5 Roman Ilich Gruber, 'Responses of Shostakovich to a Questionnaire on the Psychology of the Creative Process', in *Shostakovich and his World*, ed. Fay, pp. 32–3.
6 Irina Bobïkina, *Dmitriy Shostakovich v pis'makh i dokumentakh* (Moscow, 2000), p. 117.
7 Laurel Fay, *Shostakovich: A Life* (New York, 2000), p. 55.

8 Ibid.
9 John Riley, 'The Glivenko/Shostakovich Letters', *DSCH Society Newsletter*, 20 (1992), p. 26.
10 Wilson, *Shostakovich*, p. 74.
11 Dmitriy Sollertinsky, Lyudmila Mikheyeva, Galina Kopïtova, Ol'ga Dansker and Lyudmila Kovnatskaya, eds, *Pis'ma I. I. Sollertinskomu* (St Petersburg, 2006), Letter 8 August 1930, pp. 69–72.
12 Ibid., p. 68.
13 Ibid., pp. 69–73.
14 Galina Kopïtova, 'Poeticheskie istochniki vokal'nogo tsikla D. D. Shostakovicha. Shest' romansov na slova yaponskikh poetov', in *Dmitriy Shostakovich: Issledovaniya i materialï* (Moscow, 2011), vol. III, p. 198.
15 Ibid., pp. 192–3.

2 On the Edge of the Whirlwind

1 Laurel Fay, *Shostakovich: A Life* (New York, 2000), p. 77.
2 D. Shostakovich, 'About my Opera', published libretto, *Katerina Izmailova* (Nemirovich-Danchenko production, Moscow, 1934), p. 11.
3 Nelli Kravets, *Ryadom Velikimi: Atovm'yan i ego vremya* (Moscow, 2012), pp. 224–5.
4 See Vera Figner, *Memoirs of a Revolutionist* (1927), trans. Richard Stites (DeKalb, IL, 1991).
5 Ginzburg's two memoirs, *Into the Whirlwind* (London, 1967) and *Within the Whirlwind* (New York, 1981), are among the most vivid accounts of the Soviet Gulag during the Stalin era.
6 For the best available survey of Soviet musicians in the Gulag in English, see Inna Klause, 'Composers in the Gulag: A Preliminary Survey', in *Russian Music since 1917: Reappraisal and Rediscovery*, ed. Marina Frolova-Walker and Patrick Zuk (New York, 2017), pp. 88–217. For information on the Shostakovich family friends, see Galina Kopïtova, 'O rozhdenii i kreshchenii D. D. Shostakovicha', *Dmitriy Shostakovich: Issledovaniya i materialï* (Moscow, 2005), vol. I, pp. 5–27.
7 Sofia Khentova, 'We Live in a Time of Strong Passions and Impulsive Actions', trans. Katia Vinogradova, *DSCH Society Newsletter*, 21 (London, 1992), p. 9.

8   Dmitriy Sollertinsky, Lyudmila Mikheyeva, Galina Kopïtova, Ol'ga
    Dansker and Lyudmila Kovnatskaya, eds, *Pis'ma I. I. Sollertinskomu*
    (St Petersburg, 2006), Letter 10 March 1935, p. 155.
9   Ibid., Letter 30–31 October 1935, p. 176.
10 Sofia Khentova, 'Remembering Shostakovich: The Khentova
    Interviews. Abram Abramovich Ashkenazy', *DSCH Journal*, 20 (2004),
    p. 10.
11 Elizabeth Wilson, *Shostakovich: A Life Remembered*, rev. edn
    (London, 2006), p. 134.
12 *Pravda*, 28 January 1936, p. 3.
13 Wilson, *Shostakovich*, p. 130.
14 Isaak Glikman, *Story of a Friendship: The Letters of Dmitry Shostakovich
    to Isaak Glikman with a Commentary by Isaak Glikman*, trans. Anthony
    Phillips (London, 2001), p. 215.
15 Ibid., p. 194.
16 Fay, *Shostakovich*, p. 96.
17 Ol'ga Digonskaya, 'O Shostakovich v seredine 1930-kh: opernïe planï
    i voplosheniya (ob atributsii neizvestnogo avtografa)', *Muzïkal'naya
    akademiya*, 1 (2007), pp. 48–60.
18 Wilson, *Shostakovich*, p. 147.
19 Inna Barsova, *Nikolay Sergeyevich Zhilayev: Trudï, dni i gibel'* (Moscow,
    2008), p. 35, and Irina Bobïkina, *Dmitriy Shostakovich v pis'makh i
    dokumentakh* (Moscow, 2000), p. 153.
20 Barsova, *Nikolay Sergeyevich Zhilayev*, pp. 39–40.
21 Wilson, *Shostakovich*, pp. 148–50.
22 Leonid Maksimenkov, *Muzïka vmesto sumbura: Kompozitorï i muzïkantï
    v strane sovetov, 1917–1991. Dokumentï* (Moscow, 2013), pp. 138–9.
23 Wilson, *Shostakovich*, p. 155.
24 Ibid., p. 151.
25 Fay, *Shostakovich*, p. 103.
26 Wilson, *Shostakovich*, p. 152.
27 Fay, *Shostakovich*, p. 103.
28 Richard Taruskin, 'Public Lies and Unspeakable Truth: Interpreting
    Shostakovich's Fifth Symphony', in *Defining Russia Musically*,
    ed. Richard Taruskin (Princeton, NJ, 1997), p. 528.
29 Ibid., p. 525.

3 Civic Responsibility and Self-assertion

1 Irina Bobïkina, *Dmitriy Shostakovich v pis'makh i dokumentakh* (Moscow, 2000), p. 123.
2 Ibid., pp. 124–5.
3 Quoted in Richard Taylor, 'On Stalin's Watch: The Late-night Kremlin Screenings, October 1934 to January 1937', *Studies in Russian and Soviet Cinema*, VIII/2 (2014), p. 156.
4 Laurel Fay, *Shostakovich: A Life* (New York, 2000), p. 112.
5 Pauline Fairclough, *Classics for the Masses: Shaping Soviet Musical Identity under Lenin and Stalin* (New Haven, CT, and London, 2016), pp. 137–8.
6 Fay, *Shostakovich*, p. 117.
7 Marina Frolova-Walker, *Stalin's Music Prize: Soviet Culture and Politics* (New Haven, CT, and London, 2016), p. 52.
8 Ibid., p. 42.
9 Isaak Glikman, *Story of a Friendship: The Letters of Dmitry Shostakovich to Isaak Glikman with a Commentary by Isaak Glikman,* trans. Anthony Phillips (London, 2001), p. xxxiv.
10 Dmitriy Sollertinsky, Lyudmila Mikheyeva, Galina Kopïtova, Ol'ga Dansker and Lyudmila Kovnatskaya, eds, *Pis'ma I. I. Sollertinskomu* (St Petersburg, 2006), Letter 4 January 1942, p. 225.
11 Elizabeth Wilson, *Shostakovich: A Life Remembered*, rev. edn (London, 2006), p. 178.
12 Ibid., p. 185.
13 See Jason Caffrey, 'Shostakovich's Symphony Played by a Starving Orchestra', BBC World Service, 2 January 2016, www.bbc.co.uk, accessed 20 December 2018.
14 Dmitriy Sollertinsky et al., *Pis'ma I. I. Sollertinskomu*, Letter 28 May 1942, pp. 233–5.
15 Ibid., Letter 21 April 1942, p. 233.
16 Ibid., Letter 28 May 1942, p. 235.
17 Ibid., Letter 14 March 1943, pp. 251–2.
18 Wilson, *Shostakovich*, p. 201.
19 Fay, *Shostakovich*, p. 136.
20 Ibid., p. 137.
21 Wilson, *Shostakovich*, p. 202.

22 Glikman, *Story of a Friendship*, p. 24.

23 Fay, *Shostakovich*, pp. 145–6.

24 Ibid., p. 146.

25 Published in the *Shostakovich New Collected Works* (Moscow, 2012).

26 For Zhdanov's indictment of Zoshchenko, see Andrei Zhdanov, *Essays on Literature, Philosophy, and Music* (New York, 1950), pp. 15–45.

27 Fay, *Shostakovich*, p. 152.

28 See Leonid Maximenkov, 'Stalin and Shostakovich: Letters to a "Friend"', in *Shostakovich and his World*, ed. Laurel Fay (Princeton, NJ, 2004), pp. 43–4.

29 See John Crowfoot, Introduction to Emma Gerstein, *Moscow Memoirs*, trans. and ed. John Crowfoot (London, 2004), p. xix.

30 Vladimir Zak, 'The One Who Does Not Like Me', trans. Allan Ho and Dmitri Feofanov, *DSCH Journal*, 13 (2000), p. 9.

31 Ibid., p. 8.

32 Wilson, *Shostakovich*, p. 243.

33 Fay, *Shostakovich*, p. 164.

34 Ibid., p. 180. However, there was another side to Atovmyan's apparently altruistic publication of Shostakovich arrangements. See Ol'ga Digonskaya, 'Shostakovich, Atovmian and "Light Music": Paradoxes of Theory and Practice', paper given at the International Musicological Society Congress, Tokyo, 2016. I thank Ol'ga Digonskaya for sending me a copy of her paper.

4 Finding a Way Forward

1 Cited in Laurel Fay, *Shostakovich: A Life* (New York, 2000), p. 172.

2 Russian State Archive of Social and Political History, Moscow, fond 82 (Molotov), file 1019, pp. 4–5.

3 Cited in Fay, *Shostakovich*, p. 173.

4 See Elizabeth Wilson, *Shostakovich: A Life Remembered*, rev. edn (London, 2006), pp. 274–6 and Terry Klefstad, 'Shostakovich and the Peace Conference', *Music and Politics*, VI/2 (2012), available at https://quod.lib.umich.edu, accessed 22 December 2018.

5 Fay, *Shostakovich*, p. 175.

6 Ibid.

7 See Pauline Fairclough, 'Slava! The Official Compositions', in *The Cambridge Companion to Shostakovich*, ed. Pauline Fairclough and David Fanning (Cambridge, 2006), pp. 267–76.

8 Wilson, *Shostakovich*, p. 292.

9 Ibid., p. 287.

10 Ibid., p. 305.

11 For details, see Nelli Kravets, 'New Insight into the Tenth Symphony', in *Shostakovich in Context*, ed. Rosamund Bartlett (Oxford and New York, 2000), pp. 159–74.

12 Fay, *Shostakovich*, p. 194.

13 Vladimir Kuss and Tatiana Kozlova, 'Music Both United and Separated Them: Margarita Kuss and Dmitri Shostakovich', *DSCH Journal*, 44 (2016), pp. 14–23.

14 Fay, *Shostakovich*, p. 215.

15 Wilson, *Shostakovich*, p. 311.

16 Fay, *Shostakovich*, p. 92.

17 Wilson, *Shostakovich*, p. 316.

18 Ibid., p. 361.

19 Ibid., pp. 359–60.

20 Isaak Glikman, *Story of a Friendship: The Letters of Dmitry Shostakovich to Isaak Glikman with a Commentary by Isaak Glikman*, trans. Anthony Phillips (London, 2001), p. 79.

21 Ibid., p. 76.

22 Wilson, *Shostakovich*, p. 441.

5 The Inner Gaze

1 Galina Vishnevskaya, *Galina: A Russian Story* (London, 1986), p. 216.

2 Elizabeth Wilson, *Shostakovich: A Life Remembered*, rev. edn (London, 2006), pp. 377–8.

3 Isaak Glikman, *Story of a Friendship: The Letters of Dmitry Shostakovich to Isaak Glikman with a Commentary by Isaak Glikman*, trans. Anthony Phillips (London, 2001), p. 93.

4 Ibid., pp. 90–91.

5 Wilson, *Shostakovich*, p. 282.

6 Ibid., p. 388.

7 Laurel Fay, *Shostakovich: A Life* (New York, 2000), p. 223.

8 Ibid., p. 221.

9 Cited in Ol'ga Digonskaya, 'Shostakovich's "Lenin" Project', in *Russian Music since 1917: Reappraisal and Rediscovery*, ed. Patrick Zuk and Marina Frolova-Walker (New York, 2017), p. 288.

10 Glikman, *Story of a Friendship*, pp. 78–9.

11 Fay, *Shostakovich*, p. 226.

12 Ibid., p. 229.

13 See interview with Irina Shostakovich, *DSCH Journal*, 11 (1999), p. 9.

14 Glikman, *Story of a Friendship*, pp. 98–9.

15 Judy Kuhn, 'The String Quartets', in *The Cambridge Companion to Shostakovich*, ed. Pauline Fairclough and David Fanning (Cambridge, 2006), p. 54.

16 See André Berelowitch, 'Stenka Razin's Rebellion: The Eyewitnesses and their Blind Spot', in *From Mutual Observation to Propaganda War: Premodern Revolts in their Transnational Representations*, ed. Malte Griesse (Bielefeld, 2014), pp. 93–124.

17 Glikman, *Story of a Friendship*, p. 118.

18 Quoted in Fay, *Shostakovich*, p. 269.

19 Glikman, *Story of a Friendship*, p. 136.

20 Ibid., p. 153.

21 Wilson, *Shostakovich*, p. 258.

22 Ibid., p. 523.

23 'Kurt Sanderling on Shostakovich', *DSCH Journal*, 37 (2012), p. 10.

24 The concerto was filmed and recorded, and can now be viewed at www.youtube.com, accessed 23 December 2018.

25 Glikman, *Story of a Friendship*, pp. 140–41.

26 Cited in Peter J. Schmelz, 'Shostakovich's "Twelve-tone" Compositions and the Politics and Practice of Soviet Serialism', in *Shostakovich and his World*, ed. Laurel Fay (Princeton, NJ, 2004), p. 303.

27 Wilson, *Shostakovich*, p. 461.

28 Glikman, *Story of a Friendship*, p. 158.

29 Ibid., p. 147.

30 Fay, *Shostakovich*, p. 261.

31 Glikman, *Story of a Friendship*, pp. 160–61.

32 Fay, *Shostakovich*, p. 270.

33 Ibid., p. 263.

6 Final Years

1 Elizabeth Wilson, *Shostakovich: A Life Remembered*, rev. edn (London, 2006), p. 488.
2 Though Bartók's opening interval is not a tritone, the emphasis on tritonal intervals between the voices once the violins and cellos enter gives it the same haunting quality.
3 Laurel Fay, *Shostakovich: A Life* (New York, 2000), p. 241.
4 Wilson, *Shostakovich*, p. 491.
5 Isaak Glikman, *Story of a Friendship: The Letters of Dmitry Shostakovich to Isaak Glikman with a Commentary by Isaak Glikman*, trans. Anthony Phillips (London, 2001), p. 315.
6 Ibid.
7 DSCH, interview with Kurt Sanderling, *DSCH Journal*, 6 (1996), p. 14.
8 Isaak Glikman, *Pisma k drugu: Dmitriy Shostakovich-Isaaku Glikmanu* (Moscow and St Petersburg, 1993), p. 283.
9 Glikman, *Story of a Friendship*, p. 188.
10 Irina Shostakovich, 'An Answer to Those Who Still Abuse Shostakovich', in *A Shostakovich Casebook*, ed. Malcolm H. Brown (Bloomington, IN, 2004), p. 133.
11 Fay, *Shostakovich*, p. 278.
12 Wilson, *Shostakovich*, p. 489.
13 Fay, *Shostakovich*, p. 279.
14 Wilson, *Shostakovich*, p. 515.
15 Glikman, *Story of a Friendship*, p. 197.
16 Ivan Sokolov, 'Moving Towards an Understanding of Shostakovich's Viola Sonata', in *Contemplating Shostakovich: Life, Music and Film*, ed. Alexander Ivashkin and Andrew Kirkman (Farnham, 2012), pp. 79–96.
17 Fedor Druzhinin, *Memoirs* (Moscow, 2015), p. 153.
18 Alma Mahler, *Gustav Mahler: Memories and Letters* (London, 1968), p. 197.

Postlude

1 Elizabeth Wilson, *Shostakovich: A Life Remembered*, rev. edn (London, 2006), p. 253.

2   Script for 'Challenging the Silence' on BBC Radio 3, broadcast 14 August
    2006; available at https://soundcloud.com, accessed 24 December
    2018. I am grateful to Martin Sixsmith for sending me his script.

Select Bibliography

Ardov, Michael, *Memories of Shostakovich: Interviews with the Composer's Children by the Revd. Michael Ardov*, trans. Rosanna Kelly and Michael Meylac (London, 2004)

Barnes, Julian, *The Noise of Time* (London, 2016)

Bartlett, Rosamund, ed., *Shostakovich in Context* (Oxford and New York, 2000)

Bobïkina, Irina, *Dmitriy Shostakovich v pis'makh i dokumentakh* (Moscow, 2000)

Brown, Malcolm H., ed., *A Shostakovich Casebook* (Bloomington, IN, 2004)

Druzhinin, Fedor, *Memoirs* (Moscow, 2015)

Edmunds, Neil, ed., *Soviet Music and Society under Lenin and Stalin: The Baton and Sickle* (London, 2004)

Fairclough, Pauline, *A Soviet Credo: Shostakovich's Fourth Symphony* (Aldershot, 2006)

—, *Classics for the Masses: Shaping Soviet Musical Identity under Lenin and Stalin* (New Haven, CT, and London, 2016)

—, ed., *Shostakovich Studies 2* (Cambridge, 2010)

—, and David Fanning, eds, *The Cambridge Companion to Shostakovich* (Cambridge, 2006)

Fanning, David, *The Breath of the Symphonist: Shostakovich's Tenth* (London, 1988)

—, *Shostakovich Studies* (Cambridge, 1995)

—, *Shostakovich String Quartet No. 8* (Aldershot, 2004)

Fay, Laurel, *Shostakovich: A Life* (New York, 2000)

—, ed., *Shostakovich and his World* (Princeton, NJ, 2004)

Fitzpatrick, Sheila, *The Cultural Front: Power and Culture in Revolutionary Russia* (New York, 1992)

Frolova-Walker, Marina, *Stalin's Music Prize: Soviet Culture and Politics* (New Haven, CT, and London, 2016)

—, and Jonathan Walker, *Music and Soviet Power, 1917–1932* (Woodbridge, 2012)

Ginzburg, Evgenia, *Into the Whirlwind* (London, 1967)

—, *Within the Whirlwind* (New York, 1981)

Glikman, Isaak, *Story of a Friendship: The Letters of Dmitry Shostakovich to Isaak Glikman with a Commentary by Isaak Glikman*, trans. Anthony Phillips (London, 2001)

Hakobian, Levon, *Music of the Soviet Era: 1917–1991*, 2nd edn (London, 2017)

Ivashkin, Alexander, and Andrew Kirkman, eds, *Contemplating Shostakovich: Life, Music and Film* (Farnham, 2012)

Kelly, Catriona, and David Shepherd, *Constructing Russian Culture in the Age of Revolution, 1991–1940* (Oxford, 1998)

Khentova, Sofia, *Shostakovich: Zhizn' i tvorchestvo*, 2 vols (Leningrad, 1985–6)

—, *V mire Shostakovicha: zapis' besed o kompozitore, sostavlenie i kommentarii S. M. Khentovoy* (Moscow, 1996)

Kovnatskaya, Lyudmila, ed., *Shostakovich mezhdu mgnoveniem i vechnost'iu: Dokumentï. Materialï. Stat'i* (St Petersburg, 2000)

Kravets, Nelli, *Ryadom Velikimi: Atovm'yan i ego vremya* (Moscow, 2012)

Kuhn, Ernst, ed., *Volksfeind Dmitri Schostakowitsch: Eine Dokumentation der öffentlichen Angriffe gegen den Komponisten in der ehemaligen Sowjetunion* (Berlin, 1997)

—, *Schostakowitsch und die Folgen: Russische Musik zwischen Anpassung und Protest. Ein internationals Symposium* (Berlin, 2003)

Kuhn, Judy, *Shostakovich in Dialogue: Form, Imagery and Ideas in Quartets 1–7* (Aldershot, 2010)

Maksimenkov, Leonid, *Muzïka vmesto sumbura: Kompozitorï i muzïkantï v strane sovetov, 1917–1991. Dokumentï* (Moscow, 2013)

Malko, Nikolai, *A Certain Art* (New York, 1966)

Mikheyeva, Lyudmila, *I. I. Sollertinskiy: zhizn' i naslediye* (Leningrad, 1988)

Moshevich, Sofia, *Dmitri Shostakovich, Pianist* (Montreal and Kingston, 2004)

Rakhmanova, Marina, ed., *Shostakovich-Urtext* (Moscow, 2006)

Reichardt, Sarah, *Composing the Modern Subject: Four String Quartets by Dmitri Shostakovich* (Aldershot, 2008)

Riley, John, *Shostakovich: A Life in Film* (London, 2005)

Schmelz, Peter J., *Such Freedom, if only Musical: Unofficial Soviet Music during the Thaw* (New York, 2009)

Schwarz, Boris, *Music and Musical Life in Soviet Russia, 1917–1981*, enlarged
    edn (Bloomington, IN, 1983)
Seroff, Victor, *Dmitrii Shostakovich: The Life and Background of a Soviet
    Composer* (New York, 1947)
Sollertinsky, Dmitriy, Lyudmila Mikheyeva, Galina Kopïtova, Ol'ga
    Dansker and Lyudmila Kovnatskaya, eds, *Pis'ma I. I. Sollertinskomu*
    (St Petersburg, 2006)
Sollertinsky, Dmitrii, and Lyudmila Sollertinsky, *Pages from the Life of
    Dmitrii Shostakovich*, trans. G. Hobbs and C. Midgley (London, 1981)
Taruskin, Richard, *Defining Russia Musically: Historical and Hermeneutical
    Essays* (Princeton, NJ, 1997)
Titus, Joan, *The Early Film Music of Dmitri Shostakovich* (New York, 2016)
Vishnevskaya, Galina, *Galina: A Russian Story* (London, 1986)
Vlasova, Yekaterina, *1948 god v sovetskoy muzïke* (Moscow, 2010)
Volkov, Solomon, *Testimony: The Memoirs of Dmitrii Shostakovich*
    (New York, 1979)
Werth, Alexander, *Musical Uproar in Moscow* (London, 1949)
Widdis, Emma, *Visions of a New Land: Soviet Film from the Revolution to the
    Second World War* (New Haven, CT, and London, 2003)
Wilson, Elizabeth, *Shostakovich: A Life Remembered*, rev. edn
    (London, 2006)
Zuk, Patrick, and Marina Frolova-Walker, eds, *Russian Music since 1917:
    Reappraisal and Rediscovery* (New York, 2017)

Acknowledgements

I would like to thank Michael Leaman of Reaktion Books for commissioning this biography of Shostakovich, a project that has been a sheer joy to fulfil. I am indebted to several friends and Shostakovich colleagues for various kindnesses: Philip Ross Bullock, Olga Digonskaya, Gerard McBurney, Alan Mercer, John Pickard, Irina Shostakovich and Liza Wilson. Particular thanks are due to Olga Digonskaya and to Georgy Raskin of the Shostakovich Archive for kindly assisting me with the selection and reproduction of Shostakovich photographs, and to Irina Shostakovich for patiently answering my questions about Shostakovich, as well as granting permission for nearly all the pictures included in this book. Alan Mercer generously donated a full run of the digitized *DSCH Journal* to the University of Bristol Shostakovich Archive, an invaluable resource that has added many illuminating details to this biography. I would like to thank John Pickard for his generous interest in this biography, and for many stimulating conversations about it. Most of all, I thank my husband Richard for his support, love and friendship.

Photo Acknowledgements

The author and publishers wish to express their thanks to the below sources of illustrative material and/or permission to reproduce it:

D. D. Shostakovich Archives, Moscow, with kind permission of Irina Antonovna Shostakovich: pp. 18, 19, 24, 32, 46, 49, 51, 71, 79, 83, 86, 91, 115, 117, 118, 128, 129, 153, 163, 164, 171, 172; the *DSCH Journal*, with kind permission of Bryan Rowell: p. 110; with kind permission of Vladimir Gourevich: p. 21; with kind permission of Vladimir Kuss: p. 107; RIA Novosti / Sputnik: p. 6.